Digital SLR
POCKET GUIDE 2nd Edition

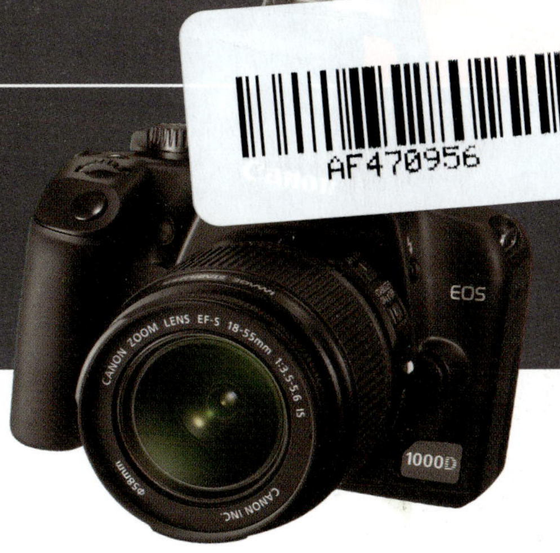

www.photoreview.com.au

INTRODUCTION:

Why Buy a DSLR Camera?

Currently, no compact digital camera ('digicam') can match the performance of even an entry-level DSLR. Although photo enthusiasts have long preferred an SLR-type camera, the latest DSLRs have much more appeal to mainstream picture-takers than earlier models.

As well as offering the benefits of higher picture quality to family photographers and travellers who record pictures they will look at time and time again, the latest entry-level DSLR cameras are also just as easy to use as a compact digicam. The basic settings are almost the same for both camera types and it's as easy to use a DSLR in point-and-shoot mode as it is a digicam.

Most recently-released DSLR cameras also include live viewing facilities that let you compose shots by viewing them on the camera's LCD. So users now have a choice: they can compose shots with the large, bright viewfinder on the camera or switch on live view and use the LCD screen. (We'll provide more information on live view shooting in Chapter 9.)

However, unlike the majority of point-and-shoot digicams, photographers with DSLR cameras can then move on to the more technical controls. Thus, a DSLR will help you to learn as you shoot and allow you to develop your expertise at your own pace.

From a technical viewpoint, DSLR cameras produce better pictures than compact digicams for several reasons:

1. Their image sensors are much larger, which means each photosite (light-capturing element) can collect more light with each exposure. (This issue is covered in Chapter 2.)

2. Because DSLR cameras have more controls and a wider range of settings, it's easier to determine what is in and out of focus in shots. (We'll look at these controls in Chapters 4, 5 and 6.)

3. Many more accessories are available when you buy a DSLR, including a much wider range of lenses plus flash units, filters and camera release triggers. Interchangeable lenses (which are covered in Chapter 3) allow you to choose the best lens for your type of shooting. You can also add new lenses cost-effectively as your requirements change. And, unlike add-on lenses for digicams, exposure levels and other aspects of imaging performance are not compromised when you change a lens.

However, some factors will deter camera buyers from purchasing a DSLR as their only camera:

1. Currently, no DSLR camera can shoot video (although we may see this facility added in the future). In the interim, most DSLR photographers carry a compact digicam or camcorder when they wish to record both stills and video clips. (A camcorder will provide the best picture quality for video clips.)

2. DSLR cameras and their lenses are usually larger and heavier than digicams. Although some models' bodies are not much larger than long-zoom digicams, the addition of one or two lenses can roughly double the amount of weight you have to carry.

3. A DSLR camera may also be more conspicuous than a digicam when you're shooting.

But these factors pale into insignificance when compared with the benefits a DSLR camera can provide in terms of better picture quality

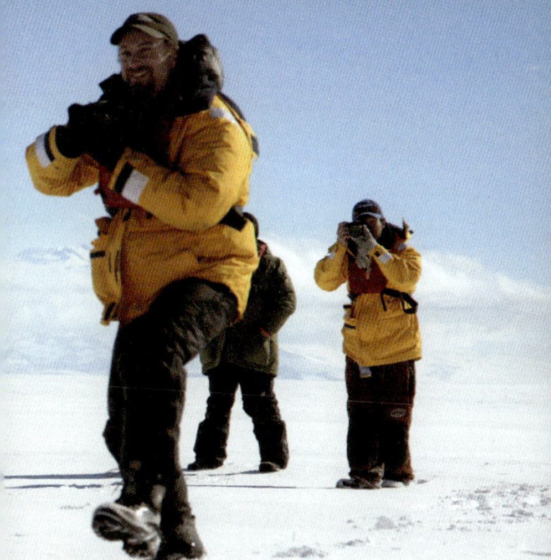

For once-in-a-lifetime situations, a digital SLR camera will provide the best picture quality and enough versatility to ensure you capture the shots.

and greatly increased shooting versatility. With a DSLR camera you can truly 'shoot like a pro'.

Deciding which DSLR equipment to buy can be difficult because there are so many choices to make. This pocket guide explains how to select a camera and lenses that will suit you and use them to their best advantage. It's written in non-technical language and presents the information you need in a way that is easy to understand.

As with other pocket guides in the Photo Review series, the second edition of the DSLR Pocket Guide is backed by Photo Review Australia magazine and website. The magazine is published quarterly and carries inspirational portfolios, buying guides and informational features on shooting and editing digital photos.

The Photo Review website (www.photoreview. com.au) publishes reviews of the latest cameras, lenses and other imaging equipment. It also provides regular new updates, information sheets of specific product types and tips on buying and using digital cameras, along with links to software you can download. You can also locate Australian retailers that offer good deals on equipment purchases and have knowledgeable staff to help you make the right buying decisions.

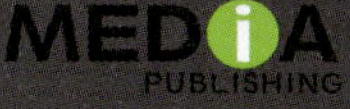

Digital SLR
POCKET GUIDE 2nd Edition

AUTHOR: Margaret Brown
mbrown@photoreview.com.au

CREATIVE DIRECTOR: Darren Waldren
dwaldren@itechne.com

SUB EDITOR: Alison Batley

PUBLISHER: David O'Sullivan
dosullivan@photoreview.com.au

ISBN 978-0-9775714-3-7
Printed by Beaver Press
Monza Satin Recycled Paper
ISO 14001 Environmental Accreditation
Distributed by NDD

Published August 2008
Media Publishing Pty Limited
ABN 86 099 172 577
Office 4 Clontarf Marina
Sandy Bay Road,
Clontarf NSW 2093 Australia
Phone: (02) 9948 8600
Email: edmail@mediapublishing.com.au
Website: www.mediapublishing.com.au

Photo Review Pocket Guides series includes Digital Camera, Printing Digital Photos, Advanced Digital Photography, and Digital Photography Pocket Guide.

MEDiA PUBLISHING

Media Publishing also publishes Photo Review Australia magazine and www.photoreview.com.au

DIGITAL SLR POCKET GUIDE   CREDITS   www.photoreview.com.au

CHAPTER 1

Choosing a DSLR Camera

When choosing a camera, the first factor to consider is the types of pictures you wish to take. Will the camera be mainly used for photographing family activities – including children's sports, family get-togethers and holidays? Or will you be using it creatively for photographing landscapes, wildlife, street scenes or other non-personal subjects? Students of photography and other photographers who wish to make photography a career or part-time income producer may have different requirements from those who simply take pictures as a rewarding and engaging hobby.

First-time buyers usually look at their budgets and set a top figure on the dollars they want to spend. While this can be a valid approach, experienced photographers tend to focus more on the camera system (body, lenses, flash and other accessories). This is better in the long term as, over time, you will probably invest more in the system than in individual camera bodies.

Choose a system whose manufacturer produces the lenses you need and, ideally, whose system is popular enough to enable you to rent unusual lenses for special situations. Some other factors to consider include:

1. How will the camera be used? Will it be used for photographing fast-moving subjects like wildlife and sports? Will it be taken into damp and dusty places? Will it be used extensively after dark?

2. Do you have existing lenses and other accessories for a 35mm SLR camera that can be used on a DSLR from the same manufacturer?

3. What do you lose by swapping from an advanced compact camera to a DLSR?

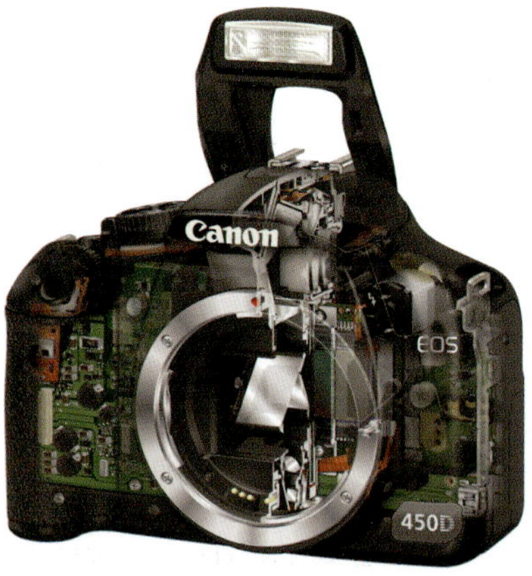

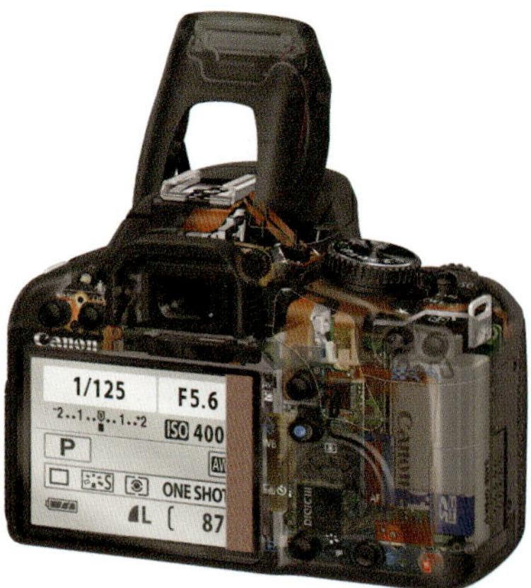

Although modern DSLR cameras are technically complex, much of this technology has been used to make them easy for photographers to operate and allow them to produce top-quality digital images.

4. What functions do you need and how easy are they to access?

5. To what extent are you prepared to edit your images?

CAMERA TYPES

The DSLR market is split into three sectors: entry-level models for everyday photographers, enthusiast or 'pro-sumer' models for people who take their photography seriously and professional models for photographers who earn a living by taking pictures. Potential camera buyers should understand the differences between the three categories in order to decide whether a camera will meet their needs and offer good value for money.

Professional DSLRs: It's easy to spot the professional cameras because they're bigger, bulkier and more complex looking – and their price tags are significantly higher. However, the main differences are usually less obvious and include build quality and functionality. Although not all pro DSLR cameras have 'full frame' (i.e.

36 x 24 mm) sensors, high sensor resolution (over 10 megapixels) is more likely to be found in pro cameras than further down the line.

Professional DSLRs are built to be used all day, every day and in a wide range of weather conditions. Consequently, they must be constructed from highly durable materials and extremely well-engineered. Most pro DSLR bodies are made from magnesium alloy, which combines a relatively light weight with toughness and durability.

Professional cameras also include high levels of dust and moisture sealing to protect the internal components. Their shutter mechanisms are typically rated for at least 300,000 cycles and they normally offer much higher continuous shooting speeds than consumer cameras. They can also capture more shots in a burst in continuous shooting mode. These factors account for a large part of their high price tags.

Pro DSLRs offer the widest range of user-adjustable controls and greatest potential for customisation of any camera. Features like Kelvin-adjustable white balance, white balance bracketing and compensation and a wide range of shutter speed, exposure settings and focusing controls are standard. Custom menus are commonly provided for saving frequently-used combinations of camera settings and adjusting various controls to suit photographers' preferences.

But don't expect a pop-up flash – or pre-set scene modes. Professional photographers require neither of these features. Instead, the mode dial on a professional camera will carry P, A, S and M settings and, although the camera will have a hot-shoe, it won't have a built-in flash. However, it will be compatible with the most sophisticated accessory and studio flash units.

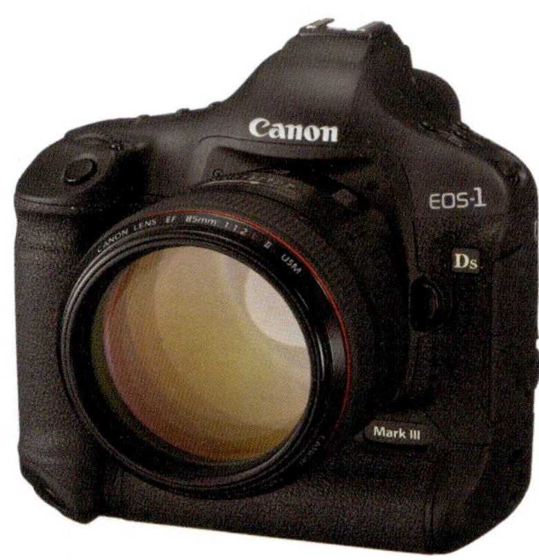

Professional cameras are large, heavy and engineered for intense usage.

Although other DSLRs will usually accept most of the manufacturer's compatible lenses and flash units, only pro DSLRs can accept and utilise the full range of accessories, including high-capacity battery packs and wireless file transmitters. Some can even download location data from a GPS unit and include it in the metadata in image files.

Enthusiast and Pro-sumer DSLRs: Sitting between the professional and enthusiast models are 'pro-sumer' DSLRs, which have some features of each type. Most pro-sumer models have 10- to 14-megapixel sensors and their bodies are made largely from metal alloy – although maybe with some polycarbonate components.

Sensor sizes vary and some cameras may lack the full dust and moisture sealing of the pro camera bodies. Most pro-sumer DSLRs have shutters that have been tested to at least 100,000 cycles and all have pop-up flash units.

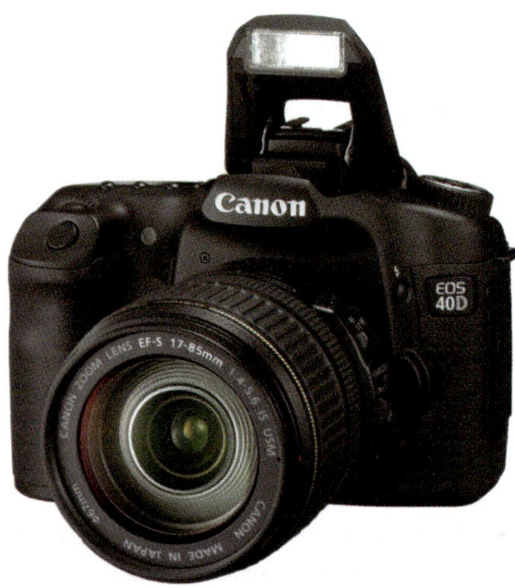

Pro-sumer cameras share features from both professional and consumer cameras.

Pro-sumer cameras offer many user-adjustable controls, although some of the more esoteric functions may be absent, the range of custom functions may be less and the internal buffer memory (for burst shooting) is usually smaller. Some pro-sumer cameras are sold as single- or twin-lens kits but most are also available as a body-only option.

Entry-Level DSLRs: At the entry level are DSLRs that are designed for everyday photographers and priced accordingly. They usually have plastic (polycarbonate) bodies that combine strength and lightness. This makes them substantially smaller and lighter than professional DSLRs and somewhat lighter than 'pro-sumer' models.

Their menu systems are more logically configured and easier to use because many functions are identical to those found in compact digicams. Many models include features like help screens and/or illustrated scene modes to help novice users learn about the manual controls and assist them to take better pictures.

Pre-set capture modes are common, usually covering Portrait, Landscape, Close-up, Action and Night Portrait modes, with other pre-sets in a Scene menu. Pop-up flash units are standard. Entry-level DSLRs usually have smaller image sensors than professional DSLRs (although they are often the same size as the sensors in 'pro-sumer' models). Resolution can vary from 6-megapixels to 14-megapixels.

Most enthusiast DSLRs are sold in kit form, with one or two matched lenses. In many cases, the supplied lenses have been designed specifically for the camera's imager and cannot be used on 35mm SLRs with the same lens mount. It's not that the lenses don't fit; the view they provide is smaller and you get vignetting

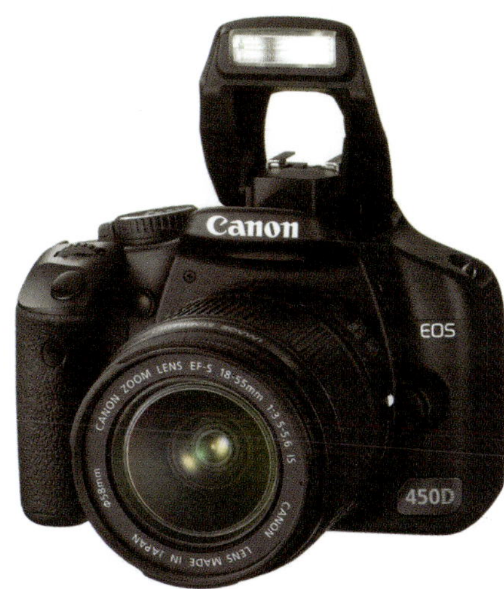

Entry-level cameras have been designed to provide all the functions keen photographers require at an affordable price point.

(darkening) of the edges of the field of view when they are used on a larger imaging area.

MATCHING CAMERA TO USER

While there may seem to be a logical correspondence between the camera types listed above and some user categories, the relationship is not necessarily straightforward and some additional features may need to be considered to achieve the best match between a photographer and a camera type. We've outlined a variety of different types of photographers with camera type suggestions below.

1. Novice Buyers of DSLR cameras usually want to learn more about photography and turn it into a rewarding pastime. Photographers in this category are often stepping up from a digicam to a DSLR or swapping from a film camera to a digital camera. Although the latter may have some photographic knowledge and expertise, their understanding of digital technology may be sketchy so they need simple ways to translate their existing knowledge to the new digital platform.

Entry-level models are ideal for these photographers, particularly if they include pre-

set scene modes and guide or help screens to explain various camera controls. Live view shooting will be particularly useful as it allows the camera to be used in the same way as a digicam for composing and capturing shots.

Cameras that use SD or SDHC cards are worth considering if you are transitioning from a digicam to a DSLR because you can use the memory cards you bought for your digicam in the new camera. DSLRs that use SD and SDHC cards are usually slightly smaller and lighter than those that use the larger CompactFlash cards.

2. Family Photographers normally look for a camera that will take better pictures than their digicams and offers greater versatility. People in this group will also focus on entry-level models that are simple enough for both parents and teenagers in the family to operate. Many purchasers will be drawn to twin lens kits (which contain both wide and tele zoom lenses), particularly if some family members are involved in active sports. A 75-300mm lens provides a great range for sports and outdoor photography, while an 18-55mm lens is ideal for indoor shots, group portraits and party photos.

3. Photo Enthusiasts upgrading from an existing film or digital SLR camera will usually look for a higher-resolution model from the same manufacturer as their existing camera in order to continue using favourite lenses (and other accessories). Many photographers in this group will focus on 'pro-sumer' models that offer higher resolution, greater functionality and better durability.

4. Outdoor Photographers and Bushwalkers need cameras that combine light weight with adequate dust- and moisture-proof construction. A 'pro-sumer' model could meet these requirements without adding too much weight to the overall camera-plus-lens package. For most photographers in this group, a single, extended-range zoom lens will be a better solution than carrying several lenses. Reducing the need to change lenses in the field will reduce the risk of dust or moisture entering the camera and also ensure their camera is always ready to use when that once-in-a-lifetime wildlife shot appears.

5. Aspiring Professional Photographers need a camera to learn their craft on. Because they will probably transition to a professional camera once their learning days are done, rugged construction is less important than having all the functions required in professional photography at their fingertips. Lens choices are also less

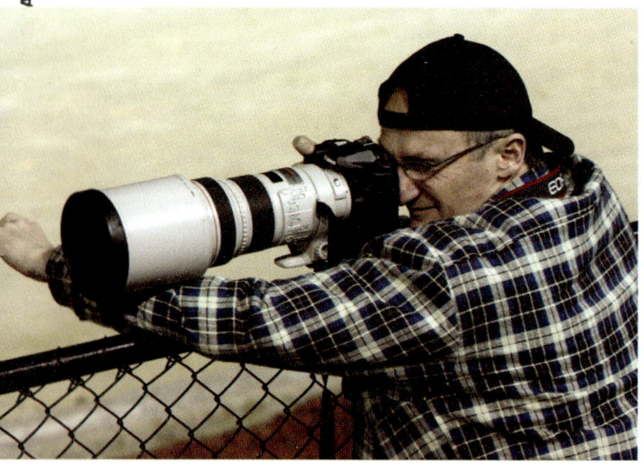

Professional photographers require a solidly-built, reliable camera but have special requirements when it comes to lenses.

relevant than having a high-performance lens that will provide high-quality pictures for their portfolio. At this stage, it may be more important to invest money in a really good lens and fit it on a secondhand 'pro-sumer' or professional camera.

HOW MANY MEGAPIXELS?

What resolution do you need in a DSLR? It largely depends on how big you want to print your pictures and how much you are likely to crop images after you've taken them. More megapixels means more detail is recorded and, consequently, you can make larger prints or apply more savage cropping.

However, paying for pixels you don't need is a waste of money. It's better to invest in a camera with a better quality lens, larger sensor and more effective image processor. The diagram above shows the optimal sensor resolution for three popular print sizes at the standard print resolution of 300 dots per inch (dpi).

Because larger prints are viewed from greater distances, resolution requirements go down as you increase print size, so there is little difference between, say, an 8-megapixel sensor and a 10-megapixel sensor. It is possible to make excellent A3 (and A3+) prints from 8- or 10-megapixel DSLR cameras and A2-sized prints from 12-megapixel or higher cameras.

HOW IMPORTANT IS BRAND LOYALTY?

If you already have a film SLR plus several lenses, should you look for a DSLR from the same manufacturer? Not necessarily. Lenses designed for 35mm cameras may not provide the best possible performance on a DSLR body with a smaller-than-35mm sensor. It's usually better to buy a camera with a matched, designed-for-digital lens.

However, if money is tight, being able to use your existing lenses on your new DSLR body is a cheap way to expand your options. But remember to take account of the crop factor that will apply when you fit the 35mm lenses to your new DSLR body (see Chapter 1). Older lenses may not provide the electronic contacts required for autofocusing. In such cases, manual focusing is the only option.

6. Professional Photographers are looking for a versatile workhorse that will keep going day after day and be usable in a wide range of situations. Different types of professionals will require different types of cameras, depending on the work they do. Studio photographers will require very high resolution and the ability to use the camera with professional studio flash systems. The ability to shoot with the camera 'tethered' to a computer may be another requirement.

Wedding photographers (especially those who work without assistants) often get by with 'pro-sumer' cameras because they are light enough to allow the photographer mobility yet their performance is close to professional standard. Many photographers will carry two cameras to provide opportunities for simultaneously shooting, say, monochrome and colour, with and without flash or with lenses of differing focal lengths.

Sports photographers require cameras with high continuous shooting speeds, large internal memories and a comfortable balance with long telephoto lenses. Many photographers in this group use fast 'prime' lenses, which are very heavy. A tripod or monopod is often required to ensure steady shots and lenses with built-in stabilisation are a must. ∎

✱ USEFUL URLS

The following websites provide additional information on the topics covered in this chapter.

www.photoreview.com.au/tips/buying/factors-to-consider-when-buying-a-dslr-camera.aspx for an overview of things you should look at when buying a digital camera.

www.photoreview.com.au/tips/buying/busting-the-megapixel-myth.aspx for information on the relevance of a camera's megapixel count.

www.photoreview.com.au/tips/buying/where-to-buy-a-digital-camera.aspx for advice on buying a digital camera.

www.normankoren.com/digital_cameras.html has useful explanations of digital camera technologies.

↗ **www.photoreview.com.au/guides for direct links.**

CHAPTER 02

Larger Sensor, Better Photos

DSLR cameras are a natural choice for anyone who wants to take the highest-quality pictures because they offer so much more than digicams in both performance and functionality. This is why a DSLR is the primary choice for a professional photographer. But everyday photographers who care about picture quality can also benefit from the following features of a DSLR:

- Plenty of user-adjustable controls, especially for lens aperture settings;
- Interchangeable lenses that cover a wide range of focal lengths;
- Faster operation and response times;
- Superior low light performance at high ISO settings
- A larger, brighter and more accurate viewfinder.

All entry-level DSLR cameras (and some 'pro-sumer' models) include a fully-automatic shooting mode for novice photographers. Many also come with a selection of scene modes that make it easy to obtain correctly-exposed pictures with common subject types, such as portraits, landscape shots, night shots and sporting action. You also get a full range of user-adjustable controls on even the most basic DSLR camera.

However, there are a few general factors to take into account before selecting a camera for your own use. In this chapter we look at the influences sensor size and resolution, image noise and dust removal can have on a camera's performance and suitability and outline some of the factors you should consider before choosing

a DSLR camera.

DSLR SENSORS

Although a high-end digicam may offer the same megapixel resolution as a DSLR camera, the individual light-capturing photosites on a DSLR's sensor are usually four to six times larger than those in a digicam's sensor. The DSLR will, therefore, have better imaging capabilities. The diagram below shows just how wide these differences can be.

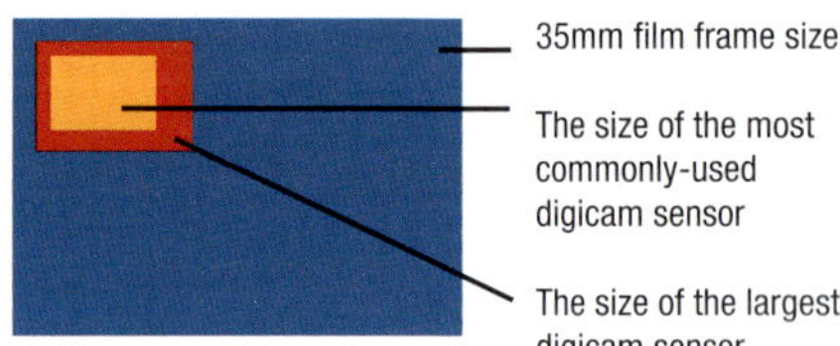

Even among DSLR cameras, sensor sizes vary and there are three commonly-used sensor sizes, shown in the diagram below.

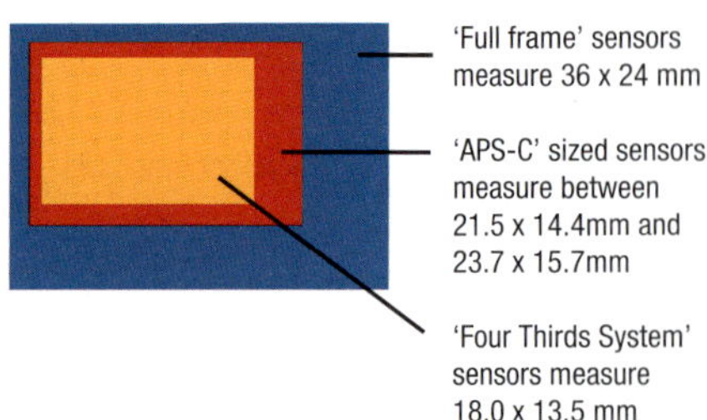

The larger the image sensor with respect to the number of photosites on it, the higher its potential light-capturing ability. More light gives the camera's image processing system more information to work with. Consequently, the camera can record a wider range of tones and reproduce colours more accurately than a compact digicam. It will also produce sharper and less grainy-looking pictures in dim lighting.

Unlike digicams, which almost universally operate with CCD (charge-coupled device) imagers, the sensors used in DSLR cameras can be one of two types: CCD or CMOS (complementary metal oxide semiconductor).

LENS MULTIPLIER FACTORS

When a lens designed for a 35mm camera is used on a camera with a smaller sensor, its effective focal length changes by a 'lens multiplier factor' (LMF) or 'crop factor' that relates to the difference in the two sensor sizes. Because the smaller sensor covers a smaller area than a 35mm camera's image circle, to find the effective focal length of any lens fitted to the camera you must multiply the 35mm focal length by the LMF.

For example, the crop factor for a camera with a 22.2 x 14.8 mm image sensor is 1.6 times. Consequently, when you fit a 50mm lens (in 35mm format) to this camera, its effective focal length changes to 50mm x 1.6, which is 80mm. Similarly, a zoom lens that would have a focal length range of 28-70mm on a 35mm camera changes its focal length to the equivalent of 44.8-112mm on the camera with the smaller sensor.

Some camera manufacturers use marginally larger sensors with a crop factor of 1.5 times. On their cameras, the 50mm lens would have a focal length equivalent to 75mm, while the 28-70mm lens would be equivalent to 42-105mm. The tiny difference in sensor size has no effect on image quality.

Manufacturers that build cameras to the specifications of the 'Four Thirds System' use even smaller sensors with a two times crop factor. On their DSLR bodies, a 50mm lens would be equivalent to 100mm, while a 28-70mm lens covers a focal length range equivalent to 56-140mm. Smaller sensors limit the wide-angle coverage of 35mm lenses, although photographers make some gains in effective focal length at the tele end of the zoom range.

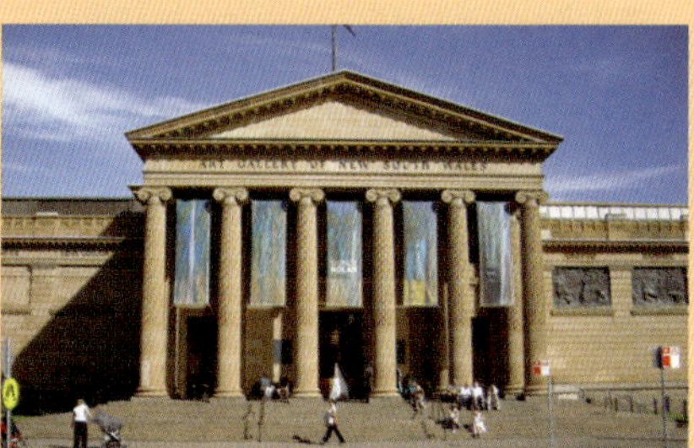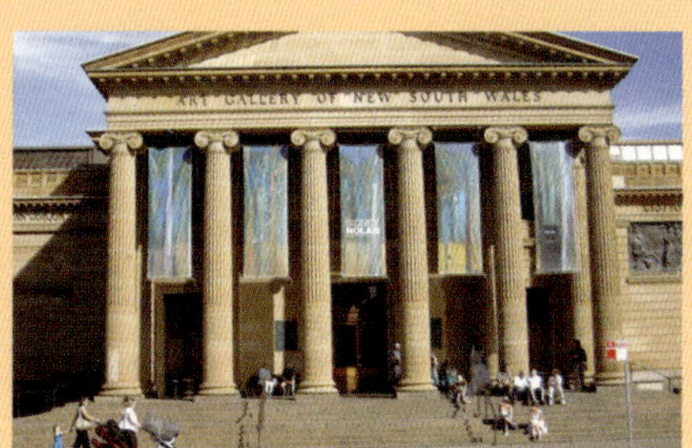

The illustrations above simulate the influence of the focal length crop factor. The coverage of a 50mm lens on a camera with a 35mm-size image sensor is shown on the left, while the same shot taken with a DSLR with a 1.6x crop factor is shown on the right.

Both types can deliver good picture quality, although CMOS chips offer lower power consumption.

CMOS imagers are favoured by manufacturers of high-end professional cameras because they can be made with more 'camera' functionality on the actual sensor chip. This makes it easier to combine high resolution with superior light-capturing capabilities. These sensors can, therefore, record digital images with a wider range of tones (from highlights to shadows), smoother gradations of colour, more accurate hues and lower image noise.

SENSOR DUST REMOVAL

Almost every DSLR camera released in recent times has come with some kind of sensor dust removal system. This technology is essential because dust that falls on the low-band-pass filter in front of the sensor can produce unattractive blotches on digital images. An example is shown below, with the dust marks circled in red.

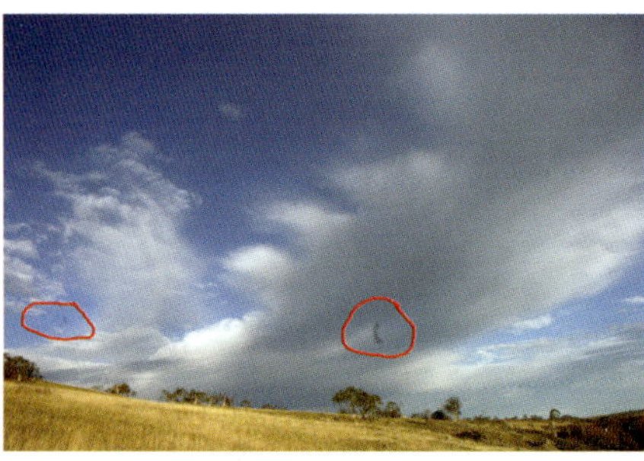

The most commonly-used dust removal systems vibrate the low-pass filter very rapidly to shake off the dust. Some manufacturers place a strip of adhesive material in the base of the camera body to trap the dust so it's not redistributed each

time the shutter is fired (which lifts then lowers the SLR mirror). Others create an airstream in the mirror box to carry dust away from the sensor.

Several manufacturers also coat the surface of the low-pass filter with anti-static material that repels dust and makes it less likely to lodge on the filter. They may also allow a little more distance between the filter and the sensor itself so any dust on the filter will be out-of-focus. This makes tiny dust specks less likely to be visible, while larger spots have softer edges and are easier to remove when the image is processed (see below).

Unfortunately, it's almost inevitable that some dust will stick if lenses are changed in damp or humid conditions so a few manufacturers have a third strategy for dealing with 'welded-on' dust. A 'dust deletion' function 'maps' the location of dust particles and allows them to be removed digitally when the image is processed with the bundled (or, occasionally, recommended) software. A combination of these systems appears to provide the most effective way to ensure digital photos are free of dust spots.

IMAGE NOISE

Image noise, which is caused by random fluctuations in the digital signal, commonly appears as graininess in the picture. In most cases, noise can only be seen when the image is enlarged substantially – at least 200 times. There are two main types of noise: luminance (or brightness) noise and colour noise. Of the two, colour noise is more objectionable because it produces an un-natural appearance. Luminance noise is more like film 'grain'.

Both types of noise are more visible in dark areas (shadows) than bright areas (highlights) in digital pictures because brighter regions are produced with a stronger signal, giving a higher

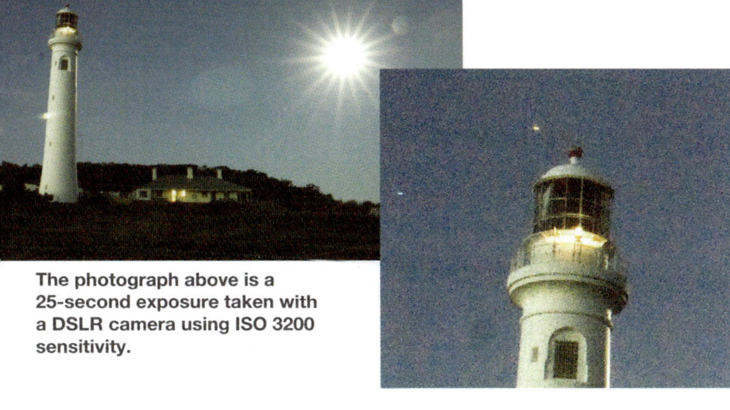

The photograph above is a 25-second exposure taken with a DSLR camera using ISO 3200 sensitivity.

An enlargement of part of the above shot shows a good example of colour noise, which shows up as coloured blotches in the image structure. A single stuck pixel (white rectangle) can be seen near the left border.

signal-to-noise ratio. The relative amount of luminance and colour noise can vary from one camera to another. However, digicams generally have higher inherent noise levels than DSLRs because of their smaller image sensors.

Almost all cameras include noise-reduction processing, particularly for exposures longer than about one second and when high ISO settings are used. DSLR cameras usually provide separate high-ISO and long exposure noise-reduction adjustments for photographers. In most cases they can be switched on and off independently and some cameras allow the 'strength' of the noise reduction processing to be adjusted by the photographer.

Sometimes you may see tiny white or coloured dots, scattered randomly throughout the image. This is a type of pattern noise, which produces 'hot' or 'stuck' pixels. The pattern is repeated in all shots taken under the same conditions. Pattern noise is more common in very long exposures, particularly when the ambient temperature is high.

Most kinds of pattern noise are easily removed by a process known as 'dark-frame subtraction' in which the camera records two images, one with the shutter open (to record the picture) and the other with the shutter closed (to record the noise). The noise pattern is then subtracted mathematically from the image data, leaving the image noise-free. The process roughly doubles the total image recording time.

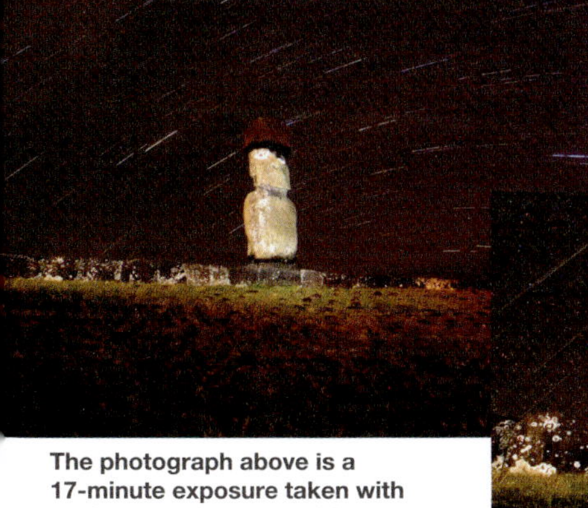

The photograph above is a 17-minute exposure taken with a DSLR camera using ISO 400 sensitivity.

An enlargement of part of the image shows the coloured dots that characterise pattern noise associated with long time exposures.

DYNAMIC RANGE

A DSLR camera can record a wider range of tones than a digicam because its sensor has larger photosites that can capture more light. With correct exposure techniques, you should also be able to record a wider range of brightness levels in each shot and even exceed the dynamic range of film.

When a photosite receives more light than it can handle, the signal overflows into adjacent photosites, which may also saturate. This usually results in blown-out highlights (e.g. white skies or snow scenes with no detail). Some cameras may also block up shadows, especially when shots are taken in JPEG format.

To prevent over-exposure of highlights, most digital photographers set the exposure compensation (see Chapter 5) on their cameras to +0.3EV, raising it to +0.7EV or even +1.0EV for snow scenes with large areas of white snow. You can usually bring out shadow detail in editing software but if no detail has been recorded in the brightly-lit parts of the image, no amount of editing can put in detail that was not recorded in the first place.

The histogram display is a useful guide for setting exposures because its shape reflects the tonal distribution in the subject. When the graph comes down to zero at or near each end of the scale, the photograph has recorded

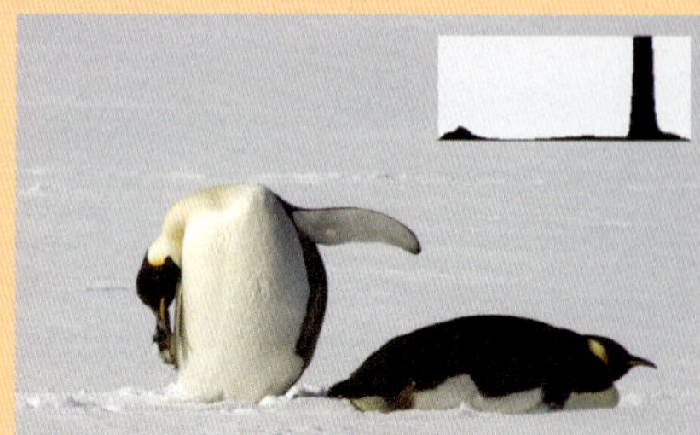

In a correctly-exposed photograph, the histogram is evenly distributed across the baseline of the graph.

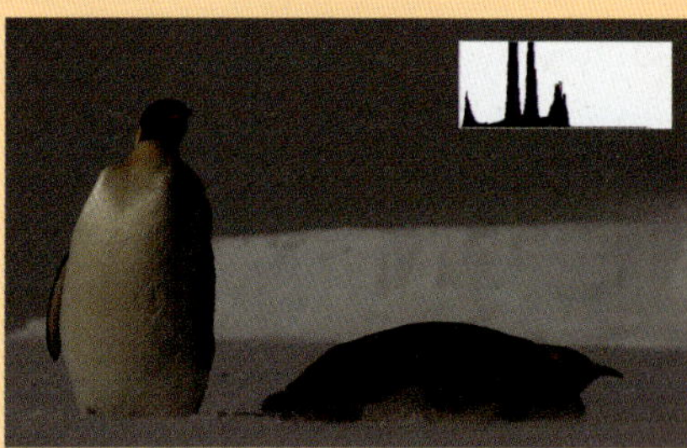

When the shot is under-exposed, the histogram is pushed to the left side of the graph and shadow detail is lost.

the full subject tonal range and highlight and shadow areas should contain detail.

When the shot is under-exposed, the histogram is pushed to the left side of the graph and shadow detail is lost.

To avoid blown-out highlights make sure the histogram does not touch the right hand end of

HOW IMPORTANT IS THE IMAGE PROCESSOR?

All digital photographs are created by processing the image data from the sensor. The degree of processing varies with the type of image files the camera creates. We'll look into

file formats in Chapter 8

Camera manufacturers like to promote the image processors they fit in both their compact digicams and DSLR cameras, largely because the image processor has a major impact on the camera's pictorial capabilities. Most

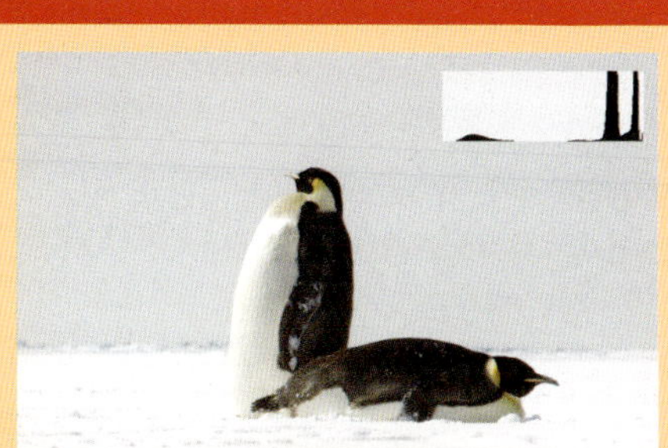

With over-exposure, the histogram is pushed to the right side of the graph and highlight detail is lost.

the scale. Blocked-up shadows can be avoided by ensuring the graph is not biased towards the left side of the scale. Use the exposure compensation function (+/-EV) to make the required adjustments. Checking the histogram to see the extent to which the exposure should be changed.

Some DSLRs include dynamic range extension settings, which use additional processing to reduce contrast at the extremes of the brightness range, thereby pulling highlights and shadows back into the brightness range that can be recorded by the sensor.

Note: shooting raw files (see Chapter 8) allows you to adjust exposure levels selectively to restore highlight or shadow detail that may have been marginal at point of capture. However, you can never recover detail that was lost through over- or under-exposure.

manufacturers even have specific brand names, such as DiG!C, Bionz, True-Pic Turbo, Venus Engine, PRIME or Expeed for their processors.

At the heart of all image processing systems are processing algorithms. These mathematical operations convert the digital data from the sensor into coloured pixels in the digital image. Processing algorithms are constantly being improved and manufacturers often indicate when a processor is updated by adding numbers or letters to the processor name.

Each manufacturer develops processing algorithms to match the performance of the image sensors they use and details of processing algorithms are closely-guarded trade secrets. However, experienced camera users can identify the often subtle differences between one manufacturer's processor and another's. Certain manufacturers have a characteristic 'look' to their cameras' shots that appeals to certain photographers.

Differences can be most easily seen in subjects with subtle tonalities, such as portraits and still life shots. If you like the 'look' of the images from one particular camera brand, it's probably because you like the subtle adjustments that result from the image processor.

Image processors also determine the camera's responsiveness and can influence the speed at which data is processed. In this area, some processors are quantifiably faster than others – and the processors in professional cameras are the speediest of all. ■

✸ USEFUL URLS

The following websites provide additional information on the topics covered in this chapter.

en.wikipedia.org/wiki/Image_sensor_format for general information on image sensors.

web.canon.jp/imaging/cmos/index-e.html for information on CMOS sensors and the advantages of 'full-frame' sensors.

www.four-thirds.org/ for more information on the Four Thirds System.

www.foveon.com for information about Foveon's sensor technology.

↗ **www.photoreview.com.au/guides for direct links.**

CHAPTER 3

Looking at Lenses

Buying a DSLR camera with one or more 'kit' lenses is an affordable way to start out your photographic adventure. However, the physical and optical designs of most of these lenses involve certain compromises to reduce weight and bulk and maintain affordability. Consequently, once the initial learning period is over, most serious photographers look at adding new lenses to their kit and/or replacing the kit lenses.

The quality of the camera's lens is as important as the size and resolution of the sensor. It's also important to match the lens to both the camera body and the types of pictures you want to take. Several factors should be taken into account when selecting lenses, the first being whether to purchase a dedicated digital lens or a lens designed for a 35mm camera.

UNDERSTANDING LENS JARGON

All lenses are specified by focal length in millimetres and maximum aperture. The aperture of a lens is the opening that allows light to pass through the lens to the image sensor. The size of the aperture is controlled by an iris diaphragm (which works in much the same way as the pupil in your eye). The ratio between the diameter of this aperture and the focal length of the lens is given in an f/number, with the maximum aperture representing the widest the iris can be opened for a particular focal length.

Aperture settings are adjustable in many cameras, with most lenses offering at least some of the following settings: f/1.4, f/2.0, f/2.8, f/4, f/5.6, f/8, f/11, f/16 and f/22. The smallest number represents the largest lens aperture. Lenses with a maximum aperture of between f/1.4 and f/2.8 allow much more light to pass

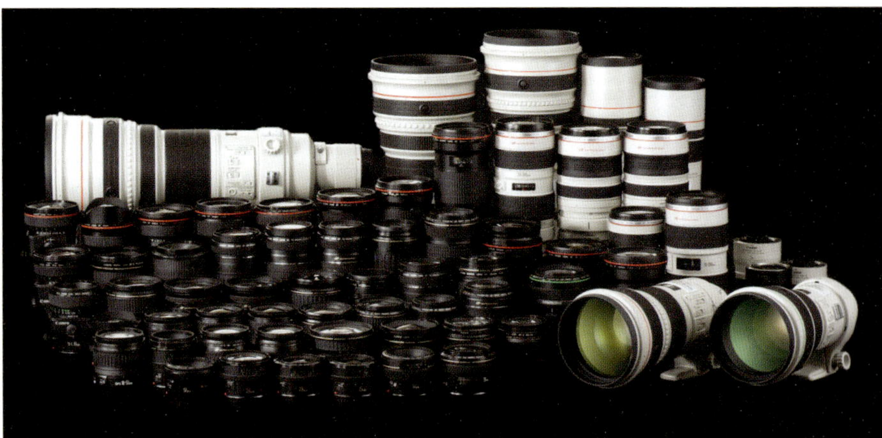

One great advantage of owning a DSLR camera is the huge range of lenses available to expand your photographic capabilities.

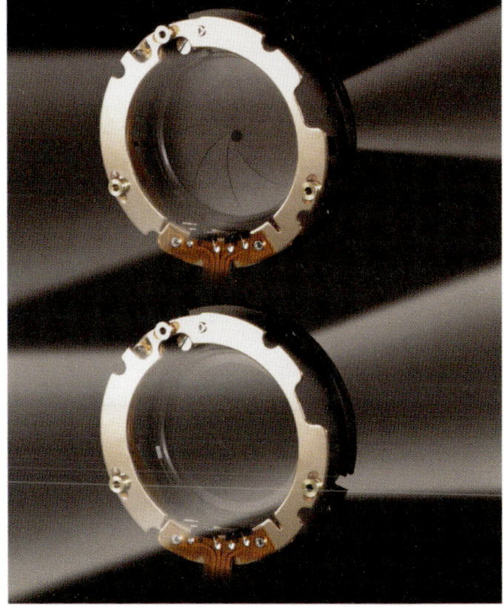

The aperture diaphragm in a lens opens and closes ('stops down') to control the amount of light reaching the image sensor. The aperture is stopped down in the top illustration, while the lower illustration shows the aperture wide open.

through them than lenses whose maximum aperture is between f/4 and f/5.6. Photographers refer to the latter as being 'slower'. Because an f/1.4 lens admits four times more light than an f/2.8 lens, it is four times 'faster'.

Manufacturers command a premium price for fast lenses because they cost more to make. They are also larger and heavier than slower lenses. The main advantages of faster lenses are greater flexibility for low-light shooting and more control over depth-of-field (how much of the subject is sharply focused).

Fast lenses allow photographers to focus on a narrow plane in the subject, leaving both the background and foreground unsharp. With slower lenses, the plane of focus is wider, making it more difficult to isolate the subject.

Zoom lenses are specified with the focal length range followed by the maximum aperture range. A 28-105mm f/4-5.6 lens, for example, has its widest field of view and maximum aperture at 28mm and f/4 and zooms to a focal length of 105mm with a maximum aperture of f/5.6. (It is common for the maximum apertures of zoom lenses to become smaller as focal length increases.)

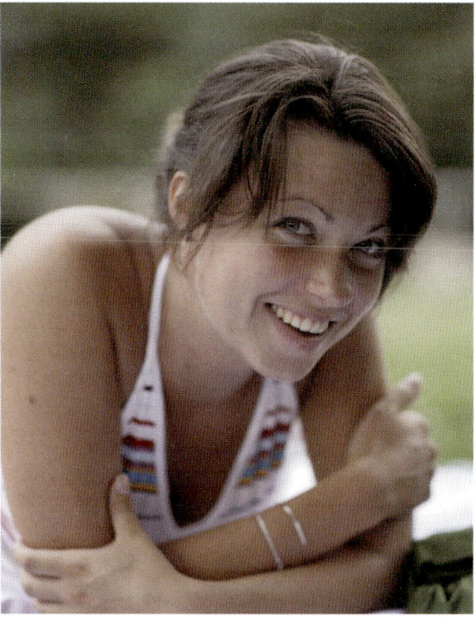

Fast telephoto lenses make it easier to shoot with a narrow depth-of-field to de-focus potentially distracting backgrounds. Taken with an 85mm lens at f/2. (Photograph supplied by Canon.)

Some zoom lenses can maintain a constant maximum aperture throughout their zoom range. A 70-200mm f/2.8 lens will allow photographers to shoot with a maximum aperture of f/2.8 all the way up to the full 200mm zoom extension. Lenses in this category are always bigger, bulkier and more expensive than those with similar focal length ranges but varying maximum apertures. However they are usually better performers.

35MM VS DIGITAL LENSES

Dedicated digital (or 'digitally-integrated') lenses are designed for imaging onto smaller sensors and can't be used with 35mm camera bodies – or DSLRs with 'full-frame' (i.e. 36 x 24mm) sensors. They can usually be identified by the letter 'D' or 'Di', although Canon uses 'S' (as in EF-S) as its identifier.

A good digital lens should provide marginally better performance on a DSLR body with an 'APS-C' sized sensor than an equivalent 35mm lens – although, in some cases, it's difficult to see much difference in actual photographs. For a 'full-frame' DSLR, regular 35mm lenses are ideal. Take account of the lens crop factor/LMF (see Chapter 2) when selecting lenses for cameras with 'APS-C' sensors. Most manufacturers include the equivalent 35mm focal length in specifications for dedicated digital lenses but you'll need to calculate the LMF for 35mm lenses that are used on these cameras. For Canon cameras, the LMF is 1.6x; for all Nikon, Pentax, Samsung and Sony DSLRs it's 1.5x, while Olympus and Panasonic DSLRs have an LMF of 2x (but can't use 35mm lenses).

Crop factor/multipliers are a mixed blessing.

Long lenses will zoom further but wide angle lenses will lose part of their ability to capture a full scene.

PRIME OR ZOOM LENSES

Which is better: a 'prime' lens that covers only one focal length or a zoom lens that ranges across many? Prime lenses are usually two or more f-stops faster than zooms. Their design tends to be simpler and the lens can be optimised to deliver outstanding quality at its designated focal length, usually across a wide range of aperture settings.

If you want top image quality, a prime lens is more likely to provide it than a zoom. For this reason, professional photographers are more likely to choose prime lenses – despite their relatively high price tags. Much of the cost of

LENS CHARACTERISTICS

Different types of lenses can impart a particular 'flavour' to pictures, making them a useful creative tool. Wide-angle lenses tend to 'spread' the subject and ultra-wide-angle lenses can introduce some interesting distortions, as shown in the illustration below.

Telephoto lenses, on the other hand, compress perspective and make objects look closer together than they actually are. They also make it easier to shoot with out-of-focus backgrounds, as shown in the illustration below.

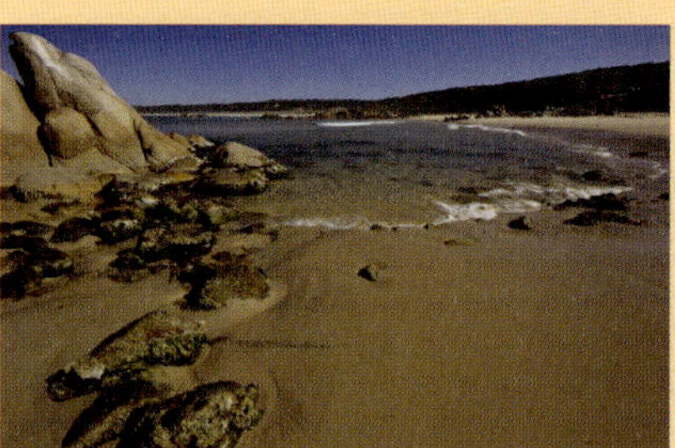

An ultra-wide shot taken with a 10mm EF-S lens at f/18.

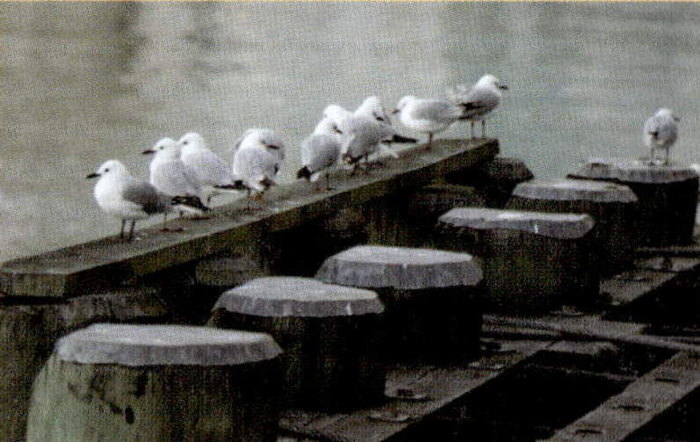

A telephoto shot taken with a 200mm lens at f/5.6.

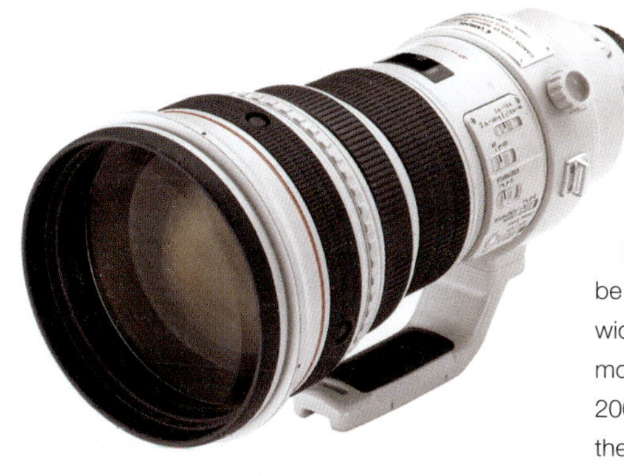

This professional-quality 400mm prime lens has a maximum aperture of f/2.8, which is very fast for its focal length. The large glass elements required add bulk and weight to the overall construction.

a prime lens is due to the high-quality glass used in the lens elements, the high precision of manufacture and the wide maximum apertures many prime lenses provide.

However, you will need a range of prime lenses to cover the focal lengths covered by even a conservative zoom – and this means a heavier camera bag to carry and higher up-front cost.

Zoom lenses are popular for their convenience and cost-effectiveness but are usually slower than prime lenses and also much more difficult to design. Many compromises must be made to cover even a moderate zoom range and zoom lenses often deliver lower image sharpness and contrast than prime lenses. Colour reproduction can also suffer. The longer the zoom range, the more compromises are required and the greater the loss of image resolution, sharpness and contrast.

Many photographers will focus their lens choices on buying one high-quality prime lens that will cover most of their shooting requirements and adding short zoom lenses to expand their shooting capabilities on either side (wide or 'tele') of the focal length of the prime lens. Shorter range zooms have fewer faults than long zooms.

For travellers, where size and weight must be minimised, a good twin lens choice is a wide standard lens (20mm or 24mm) plus a moderately wide zoom (28-105mm or 28-200mm for example). Many travellers prefer the convenience of a single, extended range zoom lens covering focal lengths from 28mm to 250mm or 300mm, despite knowing that the longer the zoom range, the more imaging performance will be compromised.

SPECIAL PURPOSE LENSES

Tilt/shift lenses have been designed to allow photographers to correct distortions related to perspective. When you photograph a tall building, the top stories appear to taper in when they are photographed with a normal or wide angle lens. In most tilt/shift lenses the range of movement is limited to +/- 8 degrees of tilt and

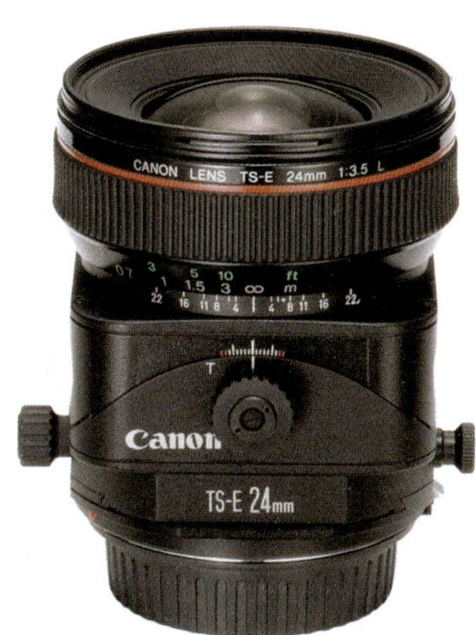

Tilt/shift lenses have adjustments that allow photographers to change the relationship of the focal plane to the subject in order to prevent rectilinear distortions.

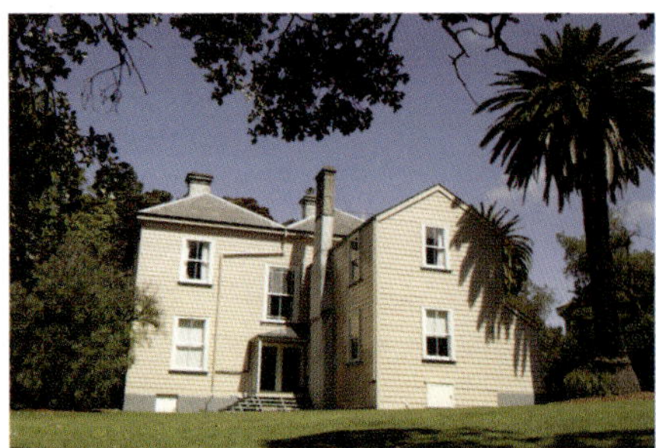

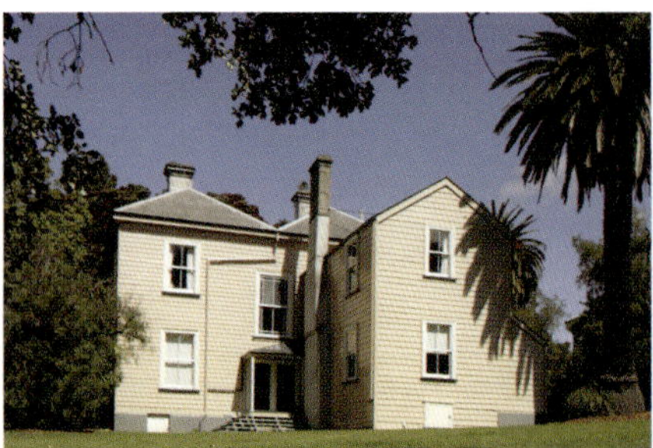

The picture on the left was taken with a normal lens. Note the converging vertical lines in the building. The picture on the right shows the effect that can be obtained with a tilt/shift lens, which allows the vertical lines to appear vertical.

+/- 11 degrees of shift, which is adequate for the majority of situations.

With a tilt/shift lens, you set the camera so its focal plane is parallel to the nearest wall of the building. Using the tilt adjustment on the lens, the front of the lens is tilted upwards to take in the top of the building, while the camera stays in position. You can keep the shape of the building rectangular and minimise the tapering at the top of the building.

The horizontal shift control on a tilt/shift lens can be used to shoot panoramas by dividing the scene into several shots. When the shots are stitched together, the distortion at the edges of sequential shots is minimised and stitching is faster, easier and more effective. Shifting can also be useful for preventing the photographer's reflection from appearing in pictures with large glass windows or mirrors.

Fish-eye lenses have ultra-wide angles of view and produce photographs with interesting distortions. They also allow very close focusing. A typical 15mm fish eye lens covers 180 degrees, which means that almost everything that is in front of the camera can be recorded, including the sky above, the ground below and surrounding objects to left and right.

While the very centre of the field is relatively undistorted, everything around it is distorted to some degree. Straight lines bulge out towards the edges of the frame, creating a strong sense of perspective. Some fish-eye lenses provide a circular field of view by cropping the corners of shots (which

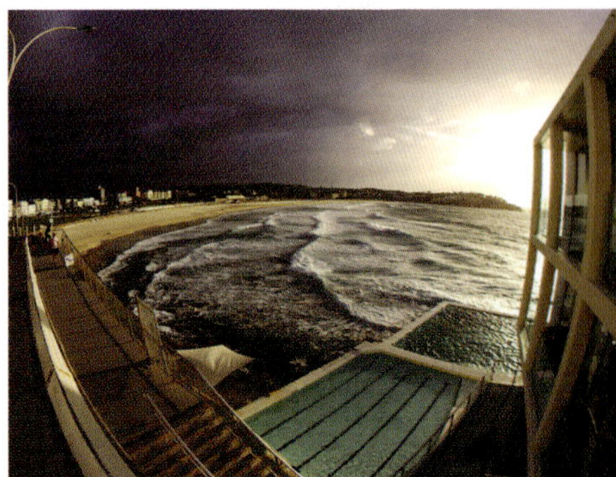

An example of a shot taken with a 15mm fisheye lens at f/5.6. (Photographed by Eugene Tan, www.aquabumps.com.)

are otherwise heavily distorted). Others cover the full frame and capitalise on the corner distortion.

TELECONVERTER AND EXTENDER LENSES

These lenses fit onto the back of a normal lens and extend its focal length by a specific factor, usually 1.5x or 2x. They're an affordable way to achieve a longer focal length with a tele lens or convert a standard 50mm into a portrait lens. However, they reduce the effective maximum aperture of the lens by the same factor as the teleconverter. For example, fitting a 1.5x teleconverter to a 200mm f/2.8 lens will extend its focal length to 300mm but reduce its maximum aperture to f/4.

On the plus side, the close focusing distance of the original lens is retained, although image magnification is increased. This

IMAGE STABILISATION OPTIONS

Camera buyers have two choices when purchasing a camera with image stabilisation. They can look for cameras that use optically-stabilised lenses or choose cameras with the stabilisation built into the camera body. Lens-based stabilisation systems are more effective when it comes to compensating for camera movements, allowing photographers to shoot with shutter speeds three to four f-stops slower than they could with unstabilised lenses. They are better equipped to counteract camera movements at longer focal lengths. The image you see in the viewfinder is also more stable.

However, when the stabilisation system is in the camera body it works by shifting the image sensor ('CCD-shift' technology). Consequently, it will be usable with any lens that is fitted to the camera. CCD-shift stabilisation systems typically provide only two to 3.5 f-stops of exposure advantage.

Most systems have separately-controlled pitch and yaw detectors, which pick up horizontal and vertical movement. Many cameras and lenses provide two IS modes. Mode 1 uses both sets of detectors, while Mode 2, which is used for panning shots, switches off the horizontal detectors.

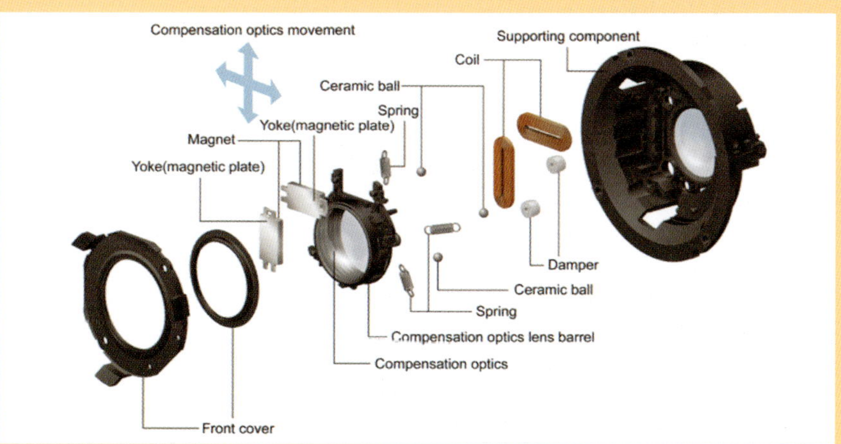

The diagram above shows the stabiliser components in an optically-stabilised lens.

can be convenient for macro photography. Teleconverters are most suitable for focal lengths of 50mm and longer and the slight loss of performance they incur can be useful for portraiture as it can give a softer look.

LENS TECHNOLOGIES

In recent years, lens manufacturers have introduced some handy new technologies, some of which are noted by additions to the name of the lens. It's useful to understand what these features are and how they work.

Image Stabilisation is commonly indicated by the letters 'IS', 'VR' (for Vibration Reduction) or 'OS' for (Optical Stabilisation).

Most systems are based on two built-in gyro sensors, which detect movement in the horizontal and vertical planes and counteract it by shifting a group of internal elements with respect to the optical axis of the lens. Many lenses have two IS settings, one for photographing stationary subjects and the other for moving subjects.

Image stabilisation is particularly useful for close-ups, when even slight camera shake can produce blurring. The stabilisation system in some IS lenses must be switched off when you mount the camera on a tripod; other lenses detect tripod mounting automatically. (Note: image stabilisation is also being built into some DSLR bodies, eliminating the need for stabilised lenses. In-the-lens systems are slightly more effective.)

Lens-incorporated Motors help to achieve fast, accurate and quiet autofocusing. In Canon's lenses the presence of this technology is denoted by 'USM' in the lens name. Nikon's technology is known as SilentWave Motor but no indication of its presence is given in the lens name. Sigma uses Hyper-Sonic Motor ('HSM') as its designation.

Internal Focusing, denoted by 'IF' indicates that the lens is focused by moving internal elements. This means the lens stays the same length and its barrel does not rotate while focusing occurs, allowing angle-critical accessories like polarisers and graduated filters to be used. Some lenses use **Rear Focusing** ('RF'), which moves only the rear lens group, to achieve the same objectives.

Apochromatic ('APO') lenses use special, low-dispersion glass to minimise chromatic aberration (the inability of a lens to focus short and long wavelengths – i.e. blue and red

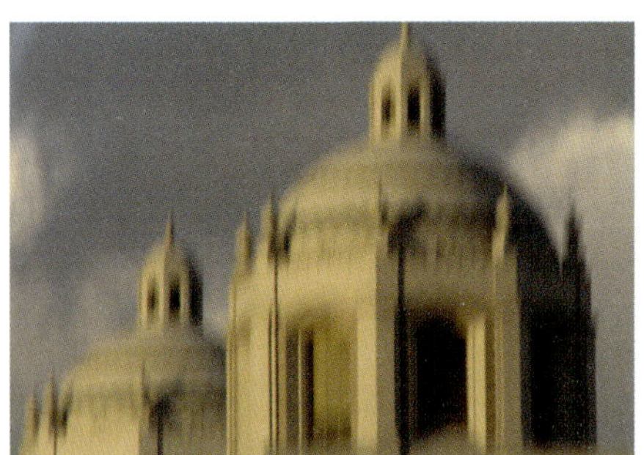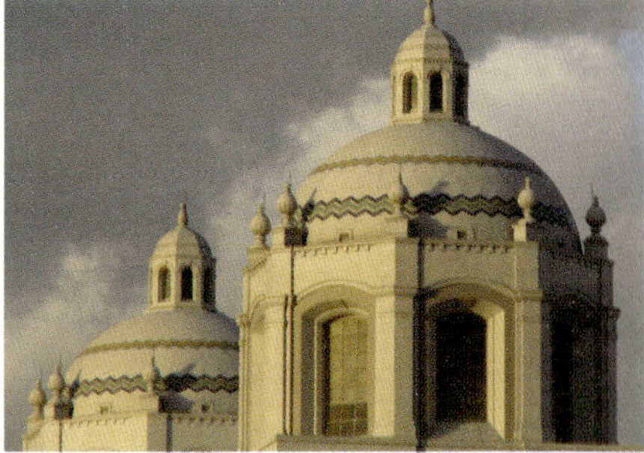

The illustrations above show what a difference an image stabiliser can make, particularly with a telephoto lens. (The image on the left is from an unstabilised lens.)

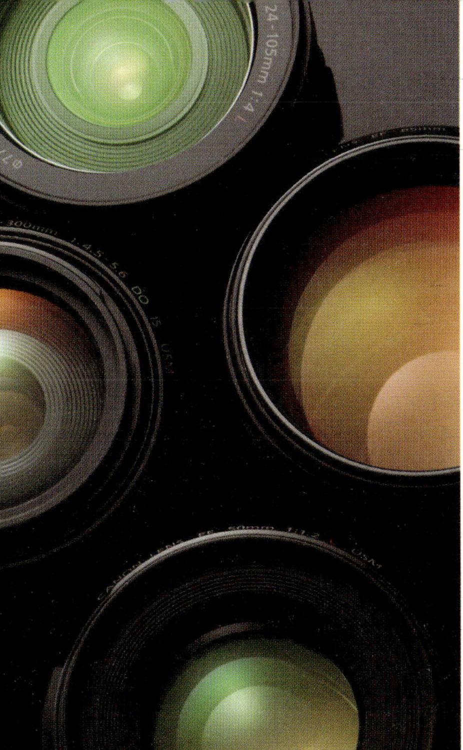

Coatings on the internal and external surfaces of the glass elements in lenses reduce reflections that can cause flare and ghosting.

light – at the same point). Such lenses can be designated 'LD' (Low dispersion), 'AD' (Anomalous dispersion), 'ED' (Extra-low dispersion) or 'UD' (Ultra-low dispersion). These types of glass are particularly popular in telephoto lenses.

Other special glass components can often be identified in lens names. The most common include **Aspherical** ('Asph' or 'ASL') elements that cause all light rays passing through the lens to converge at a single point, eliminating spherical aberration. These elements are used to reduce the number of components in the lens system and make it more compact, while also delivering improved optical performance.

Most modern lenses come with external and internal **coatings** to prevent light from being reflected back from the lens/air boundaries due to differences in refractive indices. These reflections can cause **flare** and **ghosting** when backlit subjects are photographed. Effective coatings reduce such reflections to a minimum without affecting colour reproduction.

LENS HOODS

Most lenses are supplied with clip-on hoods that shade the front element of the lens and minimise the risk of flare and ghosting. Each hood is matched to a specific lens design. Hoods for telephoto lenses are usually cylindrical, while wide angle lenses have 'petal-shaped' hoods. Using a hood ensures that the pictures you take are not compromised by a loss of contrast.

FILTERS

Filter options for DSLR cameras are many and varied as all lenses are threaded to accept screw-on filters. Clip-on filter holders can be used with most lenses, too. The most popular filters for digital photography include polarisers, graduates, soft focus filters and neutral density filters. Skylight and UV filters are unnecessary as all DSLR sensors are protected by a UV-blocking filter.

Polarisers minimise the impact of reflected light rays and are used for emphasising the blue of the sky, subduing reflections from water or glass and improving colour saturation. They are simple to use as they only need to be rotated until the desired effect is seen.

Graduated filters darken part of the picture – usually the sky. Available in several neutral density levels or in coloured form they are often used for effect but can also help to turn a fairly ordinary shot into one with more impact. (Note: the Gradient filter in editing software can be used to achieve similar effects post-capture.)

Soft focus filters are used mostly in portraiture, where they subdue wrinkles and blemishes in

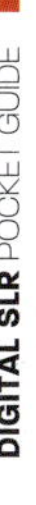

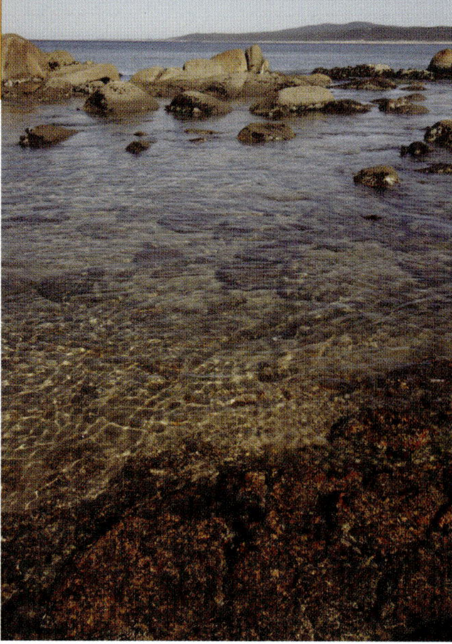
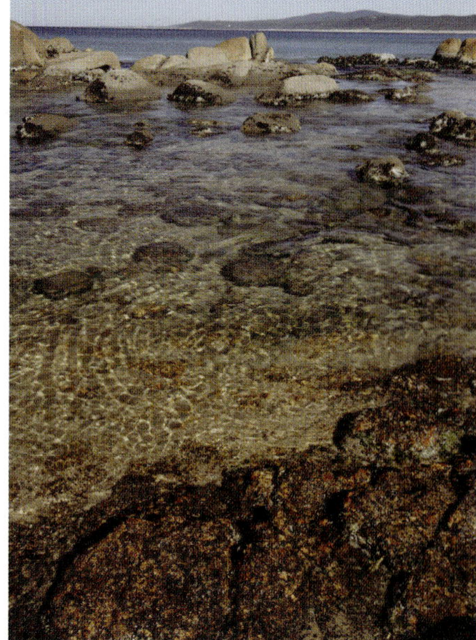

The photograph on the left was taken without a polarising filter, while the one on the right was taken with a polariser. Note how the polariser subdues the reflections from the water and allows more detail to be recorded. It also adds intensity to the colours of the sea and sky.

the subject's skin. Stronger filters can produce ethereal-looking landscape shots.

Neutral density filters reduce the amount of light entering the lens without changing its colour. They are used by photographers who want differential focusing or blurring due to long exposure times.

✷ USEFUL URLS

The following websites provide additional information on the topics covered in this chapter.

en.wikipedia.org/wiki/Photographic_filter for an excellent tutorial on photographic filters.

web.canon.jp/imaging/lens/index.html for an animated demonstration of the benefits of image stabilisation and an outline of in-lens stabilisation technology.

↗ **www.photoreview.com.au/guides for direct links.**

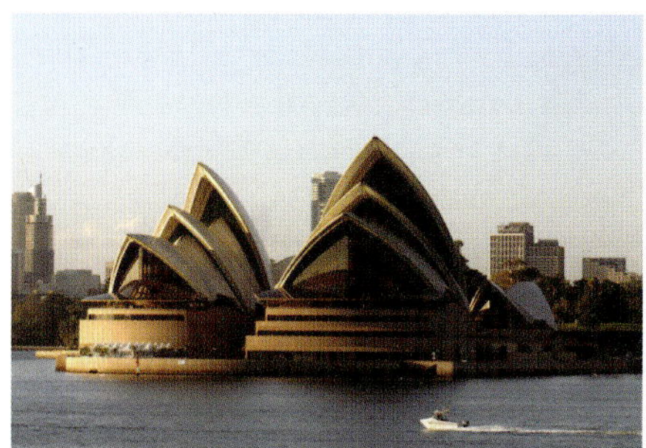
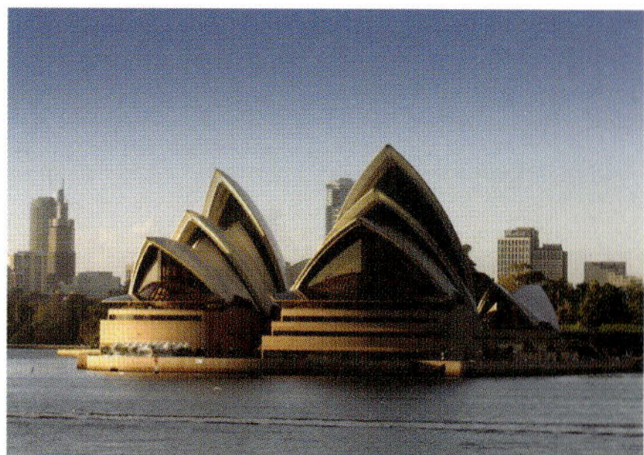

The picture on the left was taken without a graduated neutral density filter. The picture on the right was taken with one. Note the difference of tone in the sky.

CHAPTER 4

Focusing and Depth of Field

The focus control is used to make subjects look sharp in photographs. All DSLR cameras come with both manual and automatic focusing (AF) controls. The AF systems in modern DSLRs are generally fast, effective with most subjects and easy to use. Essentially there are two types of focusing, manual focusing in which the photographer focuses on the subject by turning the focusing ring on the lens and autofocusing (AF), where the camera focuses on the subject.

Manual focusing is straightforward. Provided the subject is clearly seen in the viewfinder, it should be easy to see when it is in focus and you can nudge the focusing ring slightly to correct any residual unsharpness. Focusing manually can often be quicker than autofocusing, particularly when subjects are moving rapidly either towards or away from the camera. It may also be more precise with close subjects and it allows the photographer to decide which part of the subject has the maximum sharpness.

Two types of autofocusing systems are common in digital cameras: active and passive. Active AF systems use an infrared or ultrasonic beam to measure the distance from the camera to the subject and adjust the optical system accordingly. This type of AF is common on video camcorders and some compact digicams. It is seldom found on DSLRs.

Passive AF systems analyse the light entering the camera through the lens (TTL) and set the focus accordingly. Two types are in common use, phase-detection and contrast measurement. Phase detection systems,

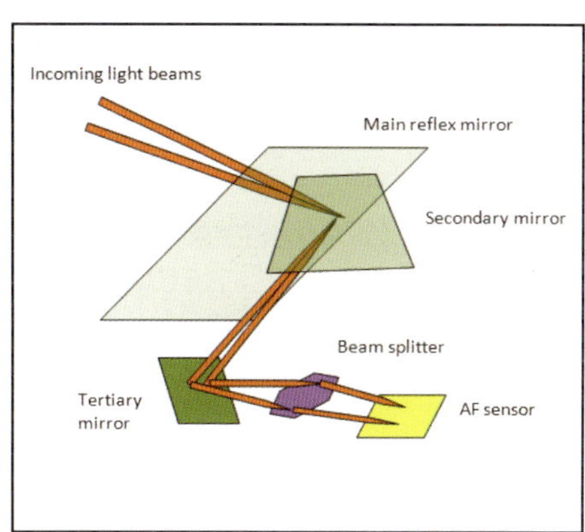

which are generally favoured for DLSR cameras, work by dividing the incoming light into pairs of images and comparing them. The system uses two optical prisms which capture the light beams passing through opposite sides of the lens.

A beam-splitting, semi-transparent mirror (or a semi-transparent area on the main reflex mirror) directs these beams down to an AF sensor, which is often located below the mirror. The two images are then analysed to find similar waveforms. The phase difference between the two images is used to determine how much the lens should be moved and in what direction. The lens motor will then move the optical components to provide correct focus.

Contrast-based AF systems, which are commonly used for the Live View mode in cameras that support this function, rely on measuring the intensity difference between adjacent pixels on the AF sensor. This intensity difference reaches a maximum when the lens is correctly focused. Although seldom used on DSLRs, contrast-based AF systems are common on digicams and video camcorders because they are fast and technologically simpler to implement.

Each type of AF system has specific weaknesses that photographers should be aware of. Active systems can't focus through window glass, mesh or bars because these impediments will reflect the IR beams. They may also fail with very close subjects. However, because they emit a beam of radiation, active systems can usually focus in total darkness, when required.

Passive systems can fail when contrast is low because they rely on subject contrast. They

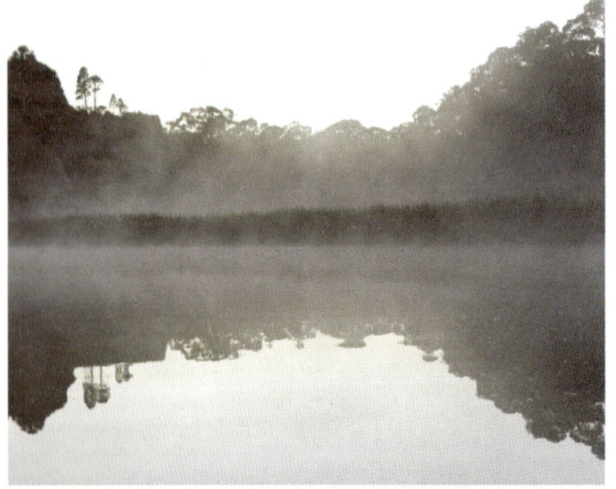

Passive autofocusing systems can fail with low-contrast subjects, such as misty scenes. (36mm focal length and ISO 400 sensitivity, 1/60 second at f/7.1.)

are most likely to fail in dim lighting or when the subject contains large areas of a single colour (sky, wall, etc.). Many cameras include an AF illuminator to overcome such problems, although it will only work with relatively close subjects.

AF SENSORS

All DSLR cameras use an array of AF area sensors to detect the signals that are used by the AF systems. Different manufacturers use different sensor patterns and many of them use a combination of rectangular and cross-type sensors for greater accuracy. Rectangular sensors provide two-dimensional intensity patterns, while cross-type sensors have a pair of rectangular sensors orientated at 90 degrees to each other.

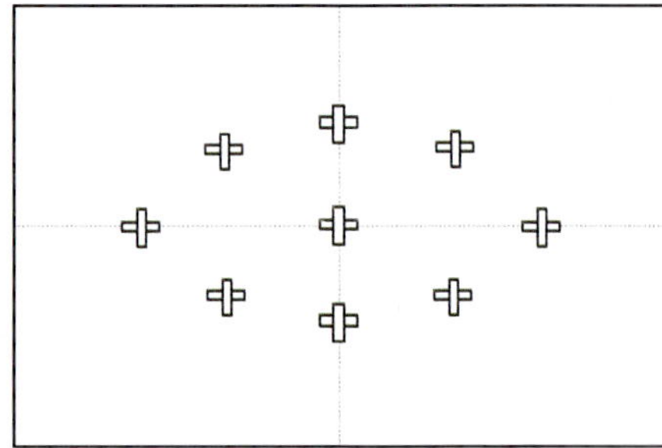

A typical AF array with nine cross-type sensors.

Cross-type sensors can recognise both vertical and horizontal movement patterns and, therefore, increase the accuracy of the AF system. Modern cameras can also analyse the subject and select the most appropriate AF area to focus on, further increasing focusing accuracy. Some sensors include a mode that will combine adjacent sensors in groups to improve focusing speed without compromising accuracy.

Some cameras allow you to select a single AF point for focusing and will normally highlight the selected area in the viewfinder. Others allow users to focus with a group of sensors. A few provide a special 'closest subject' mode that will prioritise the closest subject detected by the AF sensor array.

SINGLE AND CONTINUOUS AF

Most DSLRs offer both single (S) and continuous (C) AF modes. In single-area AF, the most frequently-used focus mode, the default setting focuses the camera in the centre of the screen. Pressing the shutter release half-way down activates the autofocus and achieves sharp focus only once. The focus is retained while the shutter button is held down, allowing the photographer to re-compose the shots while maintaining the initial focus.

In cameras with multi-area AF sensors, the AF points that achieve focus flash briefly and a focus confirmation light is displayed in the camera's viewfinder. (The exposure will also be metered at

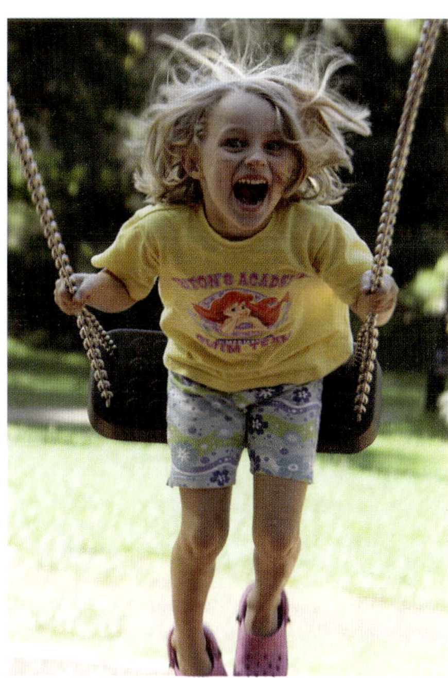

Continuous AF is effective with moving subjects because the lens is re-focused continuously. (100mm lens, 1/125 second at f/6.4.)

the focus points and shutter speed and aperture will be set in the full auto and P shooting modes.) The single AF mode will usually provide the best results for sports shots and situations where you wish to select a subject from a group

In the continuous AF mode (also known as AF servo), the camera re-focuses on the subject continuously, regardless of the position of the shutter button. This mode is handy when shooting moving subjects – provided they're not moving too quickly – but constant re-focusing consumes more battery power than the single AF mode.

If there is a brief time lag between when the shutter is pressed and when the picture is recorded, moving subjects may not be pin-sharp in this mode. Predictive and tracking AF systems have been developed to solve this problem.

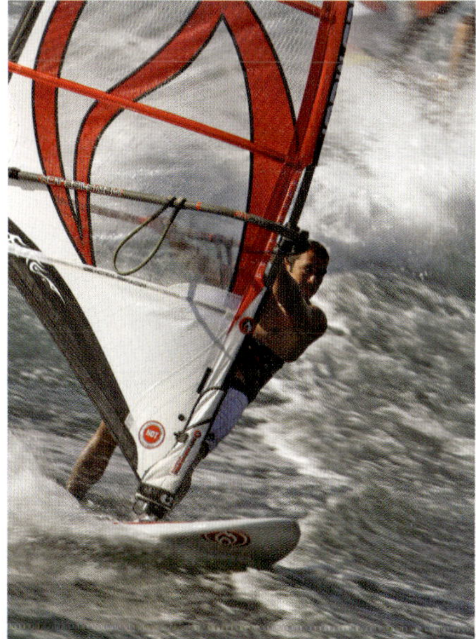

Single-servo autofocusing is best used for sports shots when you want to select a subject from a confusing background. (800mm lens, 1/125 second at f/16. Image supplied by Canon.)

PREDICTIVE FOCUS TRACKING

Many DSLR cameras include predictive focus tracking, which is useful for photographing subjects that are moving at a constant speed. When the photographer half-presses the shutter button, the AF system locks on to the subject and determines its speed and direction of motion.

A servo feedback mechanism allows the system to predict where the subject will be when the shutter button is pressed all the way down. A signal – in the form of a confirmation light or beep – indicates when focus is achieved. Note: for subjects to be sharp you need to track the subject for a second or two before taking the shot. This system won't work for subjects that are moving rapidly but erratically, such as children on swings, pets in motion and some types of sports.

AF POINT SELECTION

Most DSLR cameras allow photographers to choose which one of an array of focus points the camera will use for focus and exposure determination. The number of points varies, with some cameras offering three selectable points, others five and yet others nine – or more. The selected point lights up in the viewfinder to show photographers which AF sensor is in use. In some cameras, groups of AF points can also be selected.

Another way to select a limited range of AF sensors is to use the Spot AF mode. This focuses the camera on a small spot in the centre of the viewing screen. It is used when precise focusing is required. Unlike the AF point selection setting, this mode always focuses in the centre of the frame.

SELECTIVE FOCUSING

Controlling the width of the zone of sharp focus in a picture is one of the marks of a competent photographer. This zone can be wide or narrow, depending on the depth of field used for taking the shot. Depth of field is defined as the zone of acceptable sharpness in a photograph – or the distance in front of and behind the subject which appears to be sharp.

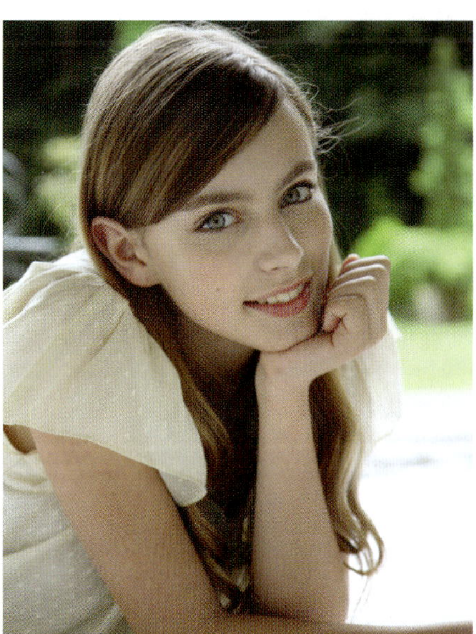

Selective focusing allows you to blur out distracting backgrounds. (55mm lens, 1/50 second at f/2.8. Image supplied by Canon.)

The size of this zone is controlled by three main factors: the lens aperture, the distance between the camera and the subject and the relationship between the lens and the size of the imaging area. In practice, it can also be influenced by how much the photograph will be magnified in the printing or viewing process and from what distance it will be viewed. These

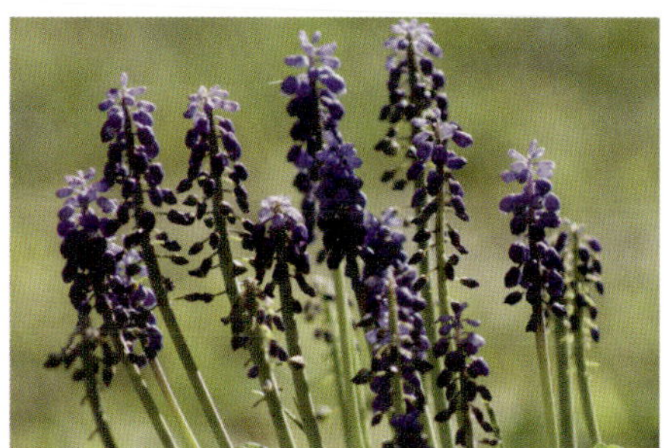

A large lens aperture (in this case f/2.8) narrows the depth of field in the image, causing the background to be blurred.

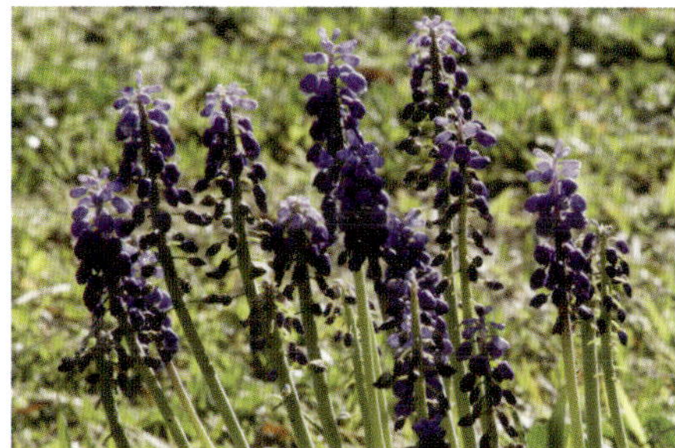

A small lens aperture (in this case f/22) widens the depth of field, allowing background details to be resolved.

factors should also be considered when taking pictures.

Large (wide) apertures produce very shallow depth of field, while small apertures make everything sharp from close to the camera to the horizon. The illustrations above show just how important the lens aperture can be in determining what is and isn't sharp in a picture – and, thus, where the viewer's eye will be directed.

Most photographers try to reduce depth of field when taking portrait shots to isolate the subject. The skill is to stop the lens down just enough to make the background fuzzy without

causing the key elements of the subject's face to be out of focus.

Start by setting the lens to its widest aperture – or one stop down if you're shooting with a focal length of 80mm or longer. If the background still looks too sharp, try moving the subject away from the background and move back so you can use a longer focal length lens. You can see how much depth of field you have in a shot before you take it by pressing the depth of field preview button on a DSLR camera. It's usually positioned low on the camera body next to the lens mount (see illustration).

Tele lenses are easier to use for selective focusing than normal or wide angle lenses. (The longer the lens focal length, the shallower the plane of focus you can achieve.) It's also easier to achieve shallow depth of field with 35mm film SLR cameras or DSLRs with 36 x 24mm ('full frame') sensors than DSLRs with smaller ('APS-C sized') sensors. With most compact digicams selective focusing for restricted depth of field is almost impossible due to their small sensor sizes, except in macro mode.

Wide angle lenses appear to have more depth of field than telephoto lenses because they include more of the area surrounding the subject. However, when the size of the subject in the

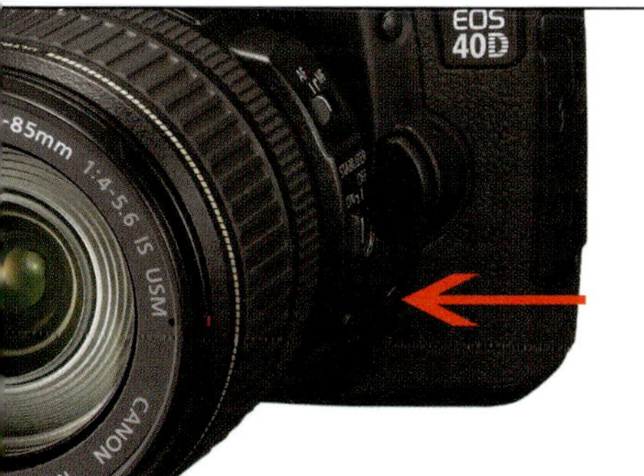

The arrow indicates the location of the depth-of-field preview button on the EOS 40D camera.

frame is identical and the other key parameters (lens aperture and sensor size) are the same, lens focal length on its own has no effect on depth of field.

Suppose you want to make as much as possible look sharp in a scenic shot? Maximum depth of field is obtained by focusing on a point known as the hyperfocal distance. If you focus on this point, everything should be sharp from half way between it and the camera right out to infinity. A quick way to set the camera to the hyperfocal distance is to focus on infinity then re-focus on the nearest point that appeared sharp when the lens was focused on infinity. If you set the lens aperture to f/11 or smaller, the subject should appear sharp from one third of the distance between the object the lens is focused on and the camera to two thirds of the distance behind the focus point. ■

✶ USEFUL URLS

The following websites provide additional information on the topics covered in this chapter.

www.photoreview.com.au/guides/digitalslr/focusing-focusing-and-depth-of-field.aspx for information on focusing and depth of field.

en.wikipedia.org/wiki/Depth_of_field for a comprehensive guide to depth of field and related topics.

web.canon.jp/imaging/enjoydslr/index.html for a general guide to using a DSLR camera.

↗ **www.photoreview.com.au/guides for direct links.**

CHAPTER 5

Exposure Metering

Exposure determination in modern cameras is largely automated although DSLRs let photographers override the camera settings and also set exposures manually. An exposure setting has two components: the lens aperture and the shutter speed (how long the light is allowed into the camera). A correct balance between them creates pictures in which all tones in the subject are recorded correctly.

All cameras include exposure meters, which measure the tones in the subject according to a selected pattern. Understanding how metering patterns work will help you to decide which one to use in different situations. Three metering patterns are used in DSLR cameras: multi-pattern evaluative (or matrix), centre-weighted average and spot. Selecting the correct pattern for the subject makes it easier to obtain the correct exposure settings.

Multi-pattern metering divides the subject area into five or more segments and individually evaluates the light levels within each segment. A microprocessor in the camera takes the readings from each segment and biases them according to the difference in overall brightness (and often contrast) within each segment and between adjacent segments. It then calculates which aperture and shutter speed settings will deliver an optimum exposure.

Some cameras also include distance information from the autofocus system and/or colour data. Multi-pattern systems are good all-rounders, providing optimal exposure settings for most types of scenes (including backlit subjects). However, because they deliver an 'averaged'

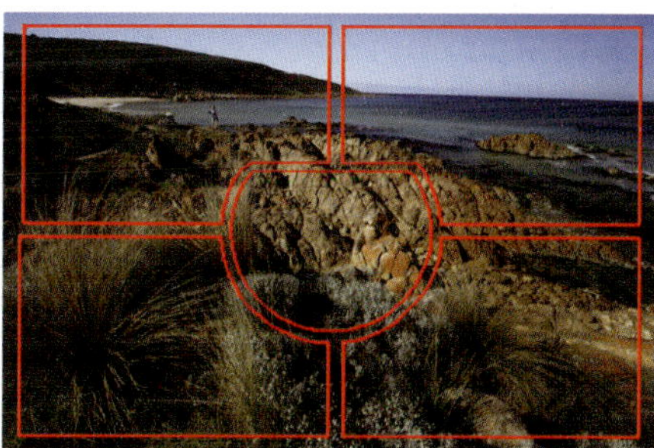

Multi-pattern metering divides the subject into a number of segments and individually measures light levels in each before integrating the data to provide a correct exposure.

exposure setting, they may not provide the best exposure for subjects with a wide dynamic range.

Centre-weighted average metering integrates readings from all over the field of view, placing more emphasis on the centre of the field. It's effective for subjects with an average brightness range where the main area of interest is central. It's not suitable for shooting bright, contrasty scenes with sand or snow or low-contrast

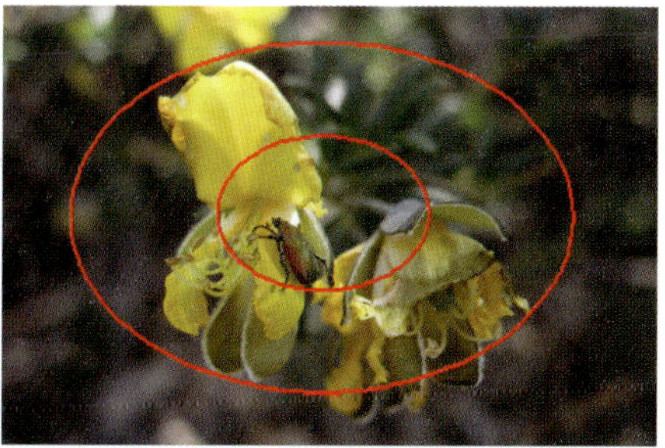

Centre-weighted average metering biases exposure levels towards the centre of the frame but takes the remainder of the frame into account.

subjects with a limited tonal range. In bright conditions, there's a tendency towards under-exposure, while poorly-lit subjects with a reduced brightness range are often over-exposed.

Spot metering takes a single reading from a small section of the field of view. In most cases, the size of the spot is expressed as a percentage of the field of view, with typical spot sizes ranging from 1% to about 4%. So-called 'partial' metering systems have slightly larger metering areas but work on the same principle.) Because areas outside the selected spot are ignored, spot and partial metering are ideal for backlit subjects.

To use a spot meter, simply centre the spot

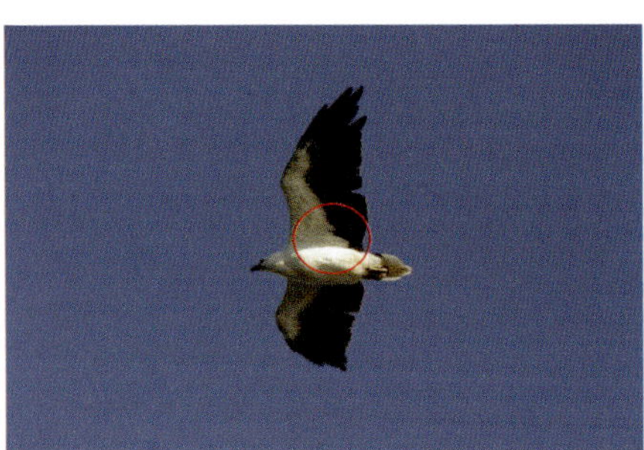

Spot metering takes a single reading from the centre of the frame. It is ideal for backlit subjects.

on the area you want to measure and press the AE lock button and/or press the shutter release half way down. This locks the exposure (and focus), allowing you to re-compose and take the shot by pressing the shutter all the way down. A spot meter can also be used to gauge the brightness range in the subject. Simply measure the brightest and darkest areas and calculate the number of stops between them. These factors make multiple spot metering the best option for digital photographers when shooting wide brightness range subjects.

EXPOSURE COMPENSATION

Exposure compensation allows photographers to alter the settings used by the camera to reduce or increase the overall exposure value. It can be used to make images look lighter or darker and also to ensure highlight or shadow detail are recorded. The control is indicated by a +/- icon, either on a button or in a menu. Pressing the button and turning the command dial adjusts the exposure level.

In most cameras up to two exposure value (EV) steps of adjustment are provided for both over- and under-exposure; usually in 1/3EV increments, although sometimes also in 1/2EV steps. To cancel exposure compensation you must re-set the control to zero.

AUTO EXPOSURE (AE) BRACKETING

The technique of bracketing, which involves taking a series of shots with slightly different camera settings from those determined by the camera's automatic measurements, is used to cover uncertainties in exposure and colour balance settings. In auto exposure bracketing (AEB), the camera produces between three and five shots, with the middle shot at the metered values and the others above and below them.

The photographer then chooses which of the shots in the series looks best and can delete the others.

Most cameras allow photographers to adjust the size of the AEB steps between +/- 2EV but you are usually required to apply the same adjustment to both over- and under-exposure. In burst or self-timer mode, the bracketed exposures are taken continuously; in single shot mode, the photographer may be required to press the shutter button for each shot. Some cameras prevent AEB with flash exposures and AEB is blocked when the shutter is set for Bulb.

AE AND AF LOCKS

Most DSLRs have an AE lock button that lets you lock the exposure on a different part of the subject from the point of focus. This control comes in handy with backlit subjects, particularly when the main subject is off-centre. In most cameras, pressing the shutter button halfway down locks both the AE (auto exposure) and AF (autofocus) settings. So, when you focus on a subject and half-press the shutter button, both focus and exposure are locked and an indicator in the viewfinder should show this to be the case.

To use AE or AF lock with off-centre subjects half-press the shutter button to capture the focus and exposure settings and hold down the AE Lock button. Then, without lifting your fingers, recompose the shot and capture it by pressing the shutter button all the way down. If you want to take more shots with the same setting, keep the AE Lock button down.

In some cameras, the position of the AE lock varies with different metering and focusing modes. With multi-pattern metering it is commonly linked with the selected focus point. With centre-weighted, partial and spot metering, it is applied at the central AF point.

FLASH PHOTOGRAPHY

Regardless of whether you have a built-in flash or hot shoe for accessory flash units, there are times when shooting with flash is either necessary or advisable. Flash is equally useful for 'freezing' moving objects, capturing shots in dim lighting and balancing the illumination on backlit subjects.

Most cameras have TTL (through-the-lens) exposure metering systems that measure the

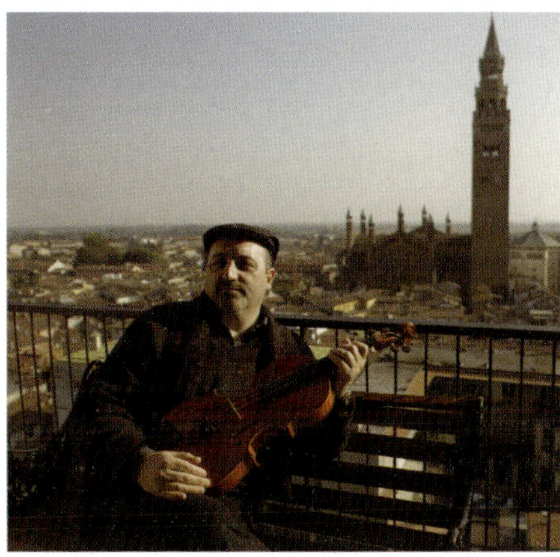

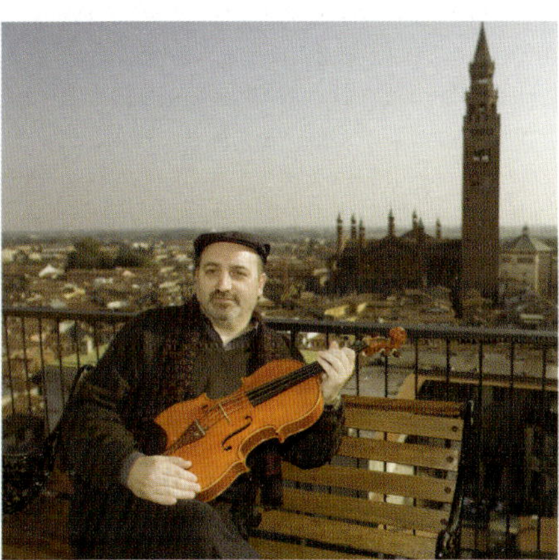

The picture at the top was taken without flash, leaving shadowed areas deficient in detail. In the shot on the below, fill-in flash adds detail and impact to the photograph. (Images supplied by Canon.)

amount of flash light reflected off the subject and shut down the flash when enough has been delivered. Consequently, it's easy for photographers to simply use the auto flash setting for all flash shots. However, better results can be obtained with a few simple strategies.

1. Reduce the flash output. Most DSLRs have a flash exposure compensation setting that lets you adjust the amount of light the flash emits. In many cases, the default setting produces harsh

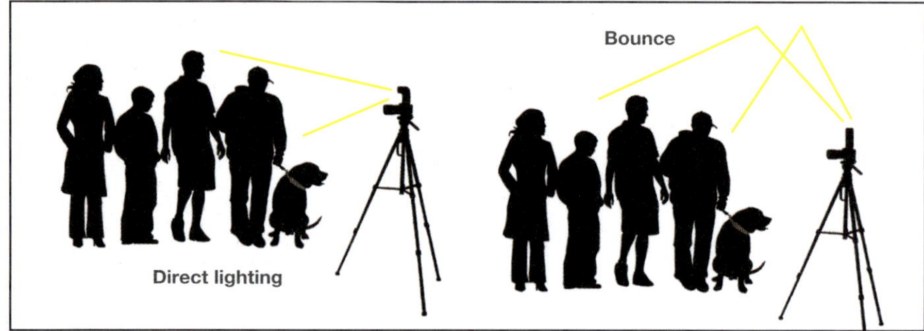

results so, as with exposure, we recommend setting the flash output level to -0.7 or even -1.0 EV. Greater reduction may be required for close subjects and some portraits, especially where softer lighting is required.

2. Bounce the flash. Many add-on flash units have adjustable heads that let you direct the light from the flash towards a ceiling or wall – or hand-held reflector card. The larger the bounce surface, the more it will diffuse the light, making it much softer when it reaches the subject. (Note that the colour of the bounce surface will affect the colour of the light hitting the subject.)

3. Use a diffuser. Many flash units can be fitted with diffusers that cover and soften the light. The effect is not as strong as bouncing but it's more controllable and there's less risk of colour casts affecting the shot.

Flash can provide some interesting effects when shooting movement. Most DSLR cameras provide both first-curtain and second-curtain flash synchronisation. First-curtain synch triggers the flash straight after the shutter opens. If the shutter remains open for a second or two and the subject is moving, although the subject's motion will be 'frozen' by the flash, any other moving light in the scene will leave trails in front of the subject as shown in the illustration on the next page.

To make the light trails appear as if they are following the moving subject, you should set the flash to second-curtain synchronisation. This fires the flash just before the shutter closes. The result is a more natural looking depiction of the motion, as shown in the illustration on the next page. The flash exposure 'freezes' the movement of the subject, regardless of how long the shutter remains open.

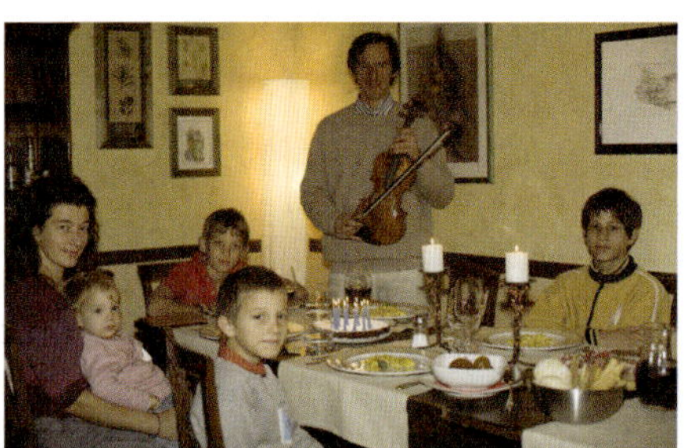
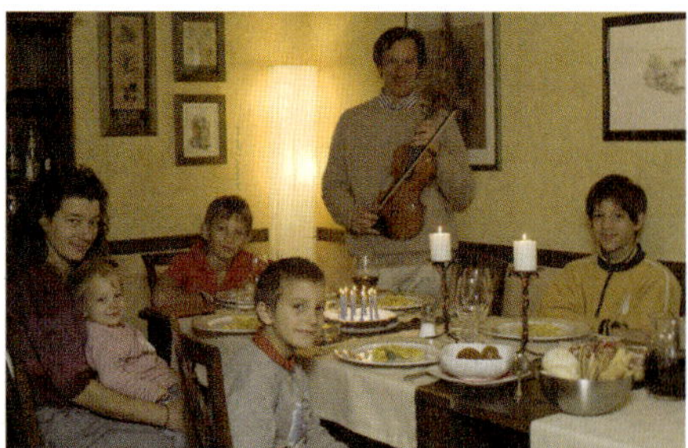

The picture on the left was taken with direct flash on the camera, whereas bounce flash was used for the one on the right. The diagrams at the top of the page show the different flash set-ups. (Images supplied by Canon.)

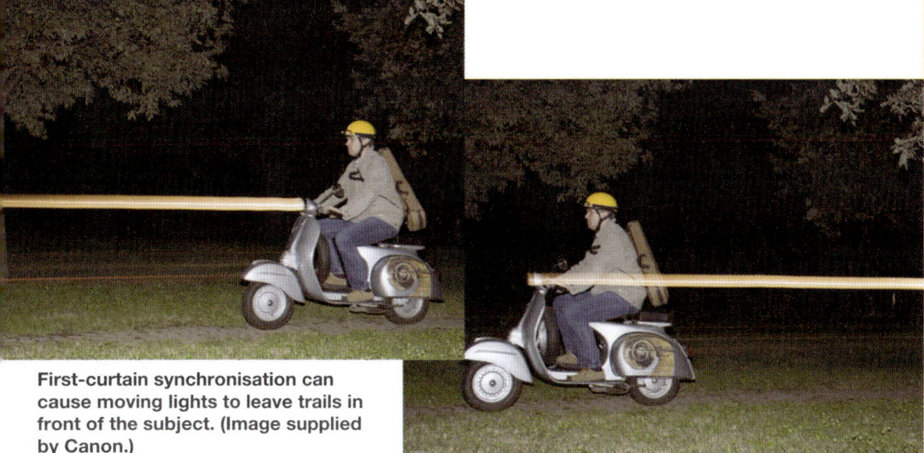

First-curtain synchronisation can cause moving lights to leave trails in front of the subject. (Image supplied by Canon.)

Second-curtain synchronisation provides a more natural-looking depiction of the subject's motion. (Image supplied by Canon.)

RED-EYE EFFECT

Most people have seen red eyes in subjects photographed with flash. The phenomenon occurs because light is emitted from electronic flash units as a very brief burst (typically milliseconds), which is too fast for the iris in the eye to contract the pupil. Consequently the flash light is focused by the lens in the eye onto the blood-rich retina at the back of the eye and reflected back to the camera. (Animals have different coloured retinas so flash shots of dogs often show green eyes, while cats can be blue, yellow or pink.)

The red-eye effect can be prevented by:

1. Using ambient light for the shot.

2. Bouncing the flash.

3. Moving the flash away from the camera's optical axis so the light hits the eye at an angle.

4. Increasing the ambient lighting so the subject's pupils close down. (This is the underlying principle behind the red-eye reduction systems built into many cameras.)

5. Having the subject look away from the camera.

6. Processing the image post-capture. Many image editors include easy red-eye removal tools. A few DSLR cameras are supplied with built-in software that can detect and correct red eyes in flash shots. This software is relatively common in compact digicams.

✱ USEFUL URLS

The following websites provide additional information on the topics covered in this chapter.

www.photoreview.com.au/guides/digitalslr/exposure-adjustments.aspx for information on exposure metering.

web.canon.jp/imaging/flashwork/index.html for a useful tutorial on the use of electronic flash.

↗ **www.photoreview.com.au/guides for direct links.**

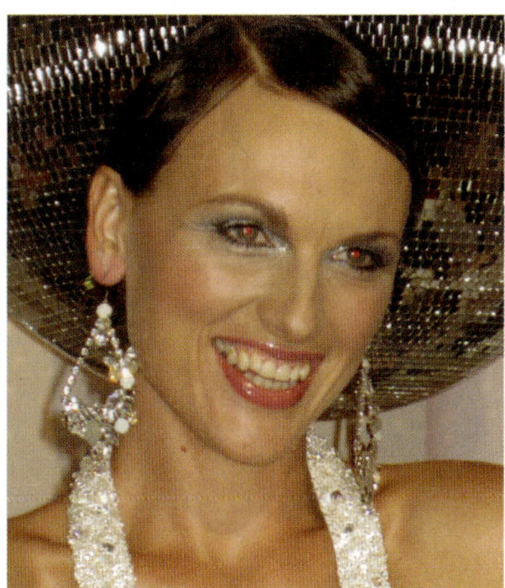

An example of the red-eye effect produced by flash light reflecting off the subject's retinas.

CHAPTER 6

Shooting Modes

Having selected the appropriate metering pattern, the next step is to choose the correct exposure mode and decide whether to rely on the camera's auto exposure (AE) system or manual controls. The main tool for engaging these settings is the mode dial.

Setting the mode dial to Auto puts the camera into 'point-and-shoot' mode, effectively handing over most controls to the camera's microprocessor. The camera sets the lens aperture, shutter speed, ISO and white balance to match the requirements of the scene it's pointed at. This mode is never found on professional cameras.

In 'P' mode, the camera also determines

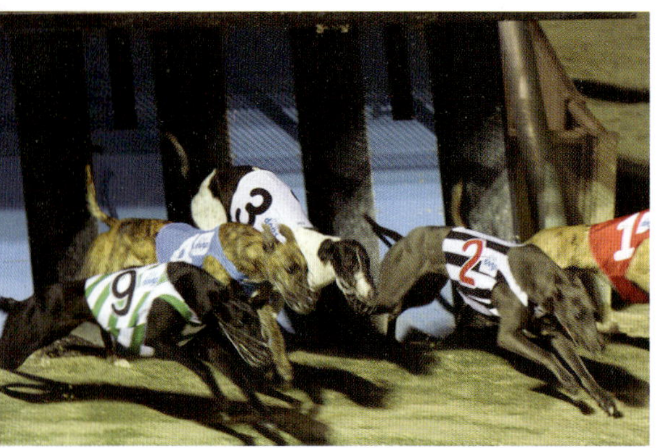

The Shutter-priority (S) mode is useful for 'freezing' fast action.(160mm focal length, ISO 1600, 1/197 second at f/3.2.)

optimal aperture and shutter speed settings for the subject. But whereas the Auto mode limits the controls the photographer can access, the P mode in most cameras lets them change either

aperture or shutter speed and will adjust the other parameter to produce the same exposure level. (This adjustment is known as 'program shift' or 'flexible program'.)

Whereas few settings are adjustable in the Auto mode, in P mode, the photographer can adjust the ISO and white balance settings and use manual focusing. Other adjustments normally blocked in full Auto mode include selection of metering patterns, exposure bracketing, continuous shooting, custom functions, colour space selection and some flash settings.

In 'A' and 'S' modes the photographer sets the aperture (A) or shutter speed (S or Tv in some cameras) and the camera adjusts the other parameter accordingly. The A mode is often used to control depth of field; large apertures produce shallow depth of field, while small apertures make everything sharp from close to the camera to the horizon.

The S mode is used to freeze action or produce intentional blurring in shots of moving subjects. Select fast shutter speeds to freeze action, as shown in the illustration to the left. Slow shutter speeds can be used to 'liquefy' flowing water, as shown in the illustration on page 37.

Manual ('M') mode gives photographers full control over both aperture and shutter speed. The A, S and M modes provide full access to all camera settings (except exposure compensation in M mode).

Camera manufacturers have differing approaches to mode dial design, some of which are shown on the next page.

The mode dials on Canon's entry-level and

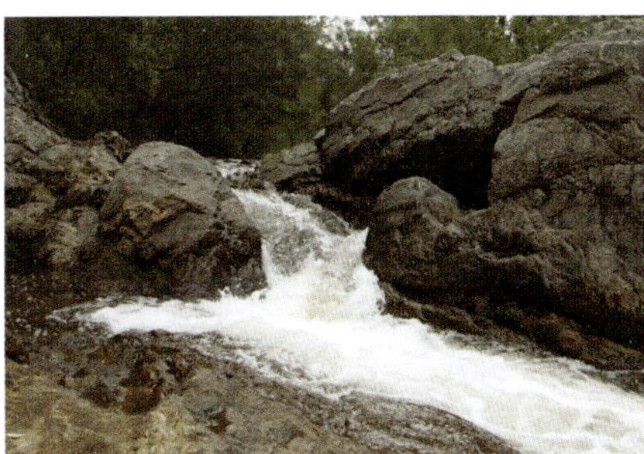

Flowing water photographed with a shutter speed of 1/1000 second at f/7.1, showing the effect of 'freezing' the motion of the water.

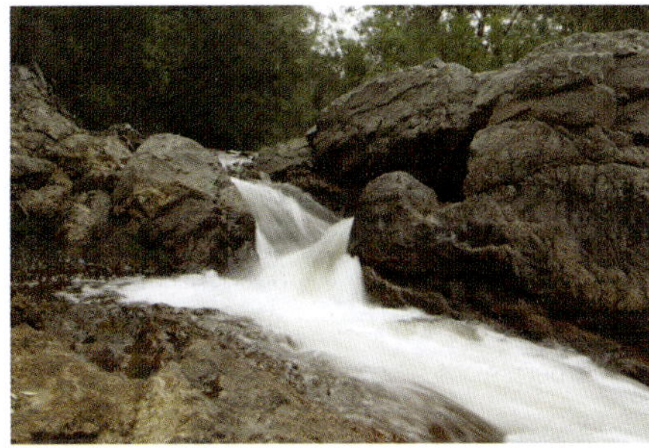

The same subject photographed with a shutter speed of 1/6 second at f/18.

pro-sumer DSLRs are split into two zones: the Basic Zone containing the Auto setting (green rectangle) and the various scene pre-sets and the Creative Zone with the P, Tv (shutter priority), Av (aperture priority) and M settings. Canon adds an 'A-DEP' shooting mode, which sets the camera to record a wide depth of field in the shot. The camera uses data from nine AF sensor points to determine the nearest and most distant parts of the subject then selects a lens aperture that ensures they will be sharply imaged. This mode is handy for landscapes and group shots.

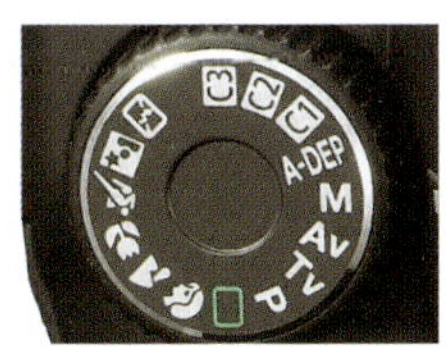

The mode dial on Nikon's entry-level DSLRs uses a grey background to distinguish between the P, A, S and M shooting modes and the Auto mode and scene pre-sets.

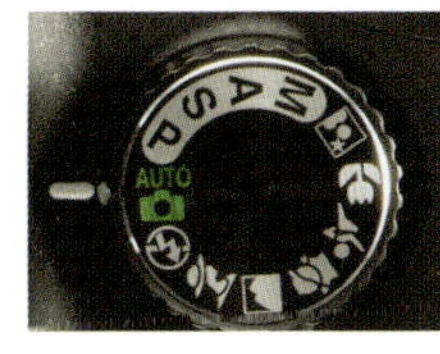

The latest Pentax DSLRs include two additional modes: a dedicated 'Sv' mode that prioritises ISO settings and enables the camera to adjust other parameters automatically and a 'TAv' mode, which lets photographers set both the aperture and shutter speed while the camera will adjust the ISO setting. The User mode denotes a custom memory bank where photographers can store groups of camera settings. The B setting is for Bulb exposures in which the shutter remains open as long as the shutter release is held down. The three icons below the mode dial are for metering pattern settings.

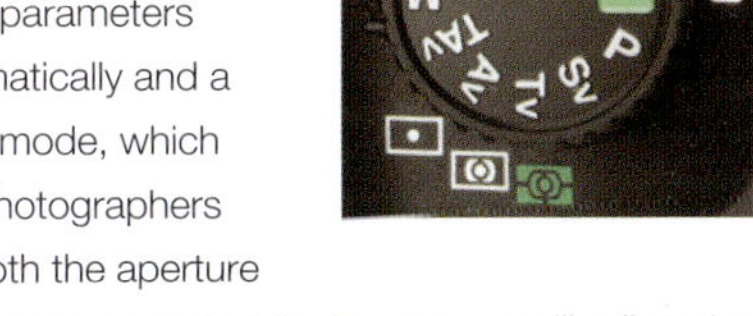

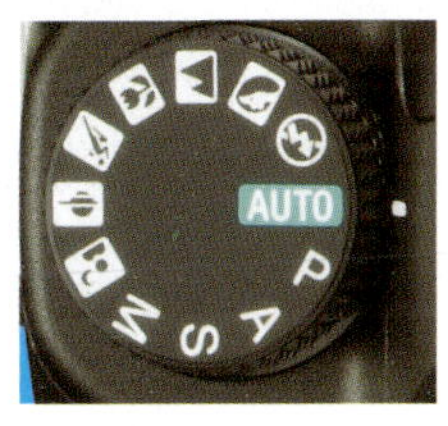

The mode dial on Sony's A200 and A350 models are identical and contain the standard Auto, P, A, S and M shooting modes and a selection of frequently-used scene pre-sets. Use of icons for the scene modes is the only distinction between them and the P, A, S and M settings.

37

Scene Mode	What it Does	When to Use It
Portrait	Selects the widest practical lens aperture to blur the background. May enhance skin tones.	For selective focusing where you want to isolate a subject from a potentially distracting background.
Landscape	Sets focus to infinity and sets a small lens aperture. May increase sharpness and saturation and/or enhance blues and greens.	For distant subjects where maximum depth of field is required.
Sports/Action	Selects a fast shutter speed and wide lens aperture plus focus tracking (if available). May set high ISO value. Flash is activated if required.	For moving subjects.
Close-up	Sets the closest focus for the selected focal length. May also set high colour saturation.	For close subjects
Night Portrait	Sets a slow shutter speed and red-eye reduction flash (if available). May also enhance skin tones.	For shots of people after sundown, where a natural-looking balance between subject and background is required. A tripod may be needed to prevent camera shake.
Flash Off	Switches the flash to off and shooting mode to auto.	For available-light shots when flash is not wanted.
Children and Pets	Selects a fast shutter speed and high ISO setting to 'freeze' movement. Other controls remain automatic.	For fast-moving subjects when flash may be acceptable.

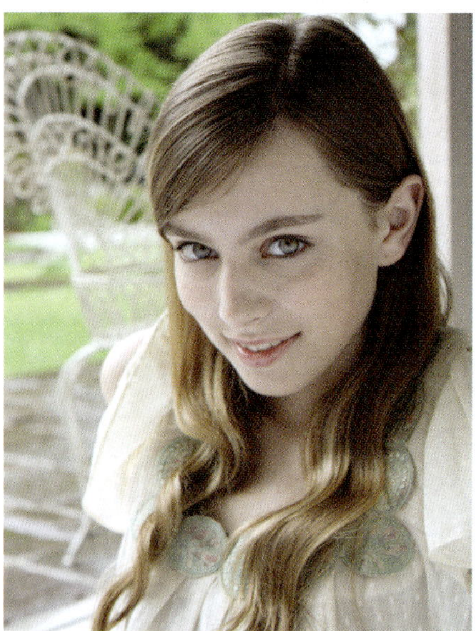

The portrait mode sets a wide lens aperture to isolate the subject from the background. (40mm lens, 1/40 second at f/ 4.0. Photograph sourced from Canon.)

SCENE PRE-SETS

Entry-level DSLRs (and some 'pro-sumer' models) provide a variety of pre-set 'scene' modes that help novice users to choose the appropriate camera settings for different subject types. The most common scene mode settings are portrait, landscape, sports, close-up and night portrait. Other modes may include: fireworks, sunset/ sunrise, night scene, beach & snow, children & pets, candlelight and document/text.

Interestingly, the adjustments used by one manufacturer may not be the same as those used by another – although they will be similar for the same scene type. Cameras from the same manufacturer may also vary when new models are introduced.

The table above shows how the more popular scene modes work and when to use them. Use them with discretion because some of the subsidiary adjustments (such as increasing saturation or boosting blue and green) may not be appropriate for your subject.

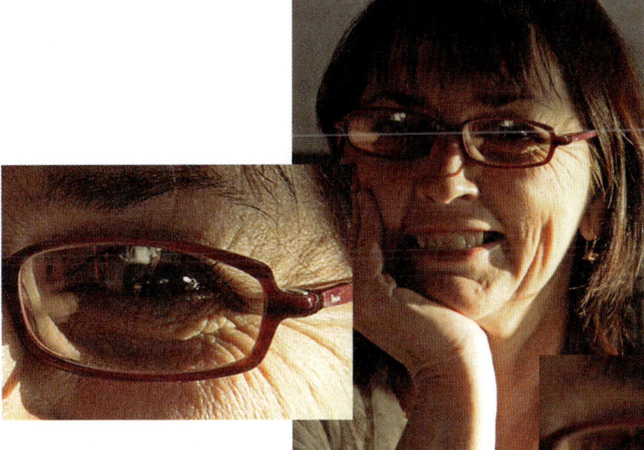

These pictures above show the effect of sharpness adjustments. The central image is the original photograph, while an enlarged section of a sharpened version of the image can be seen on the left and a softened version on the right. (Adjustments have been exaggerated to demonstrate the effects of each setting.)

IMAGE TONE ADJUSTMENTS

Most DSLRs have a special set of 'picture styles' that enable users to fine-tune the sharpness, contrast, colour saturation and colour 'tone' (or hue) settings in their digital images before shooting. As a rule, these controls can only be used in the P, A, S and M shooting modes. Up to five levels of adjustment are provided for each parameter and some cameras can 'memorise' up to three sets of parameter adjustments and store them in Custom memory banks for future use.

Sharpness adjustments work mainly on edges and allow photographers to sharpen or 'soften' their shots. Contrast and saturation (colour vividness) adjustments are similar, with the minus settings reducing and the plus settings increasing the selected parameter.

Colour tone adjustments are used mainly for tweaking the camera's colour reproduction system to produce better-looking skin tones. The minus settings in this parameter make skin tones a little redder, while the plus settings bias them more towards yellow.

Canon's Picture Style system is a variant of parameter adjustments, which allows photographers to match image colour and tonal reproduction to certain requirements.

The table below shows the adjustments made to saturation and sharpness in each of the Picture Style settings.

The Monochrome setting has been designed

Picture Style	Saturation	Sharpness
Standard	High	Moderately high
Portrait	Moderately High	Moderately Low
Landscape	High green / blue	High
Neutral	Low	None
Faithful	Low	None
Monochrome	None	Moderately high

specifically for recording B&W or sepia-toned pictures. Raw images captured with this setting can be converted back to colour with the bundled software – although JPEGs can not.

The main problem with all parameter

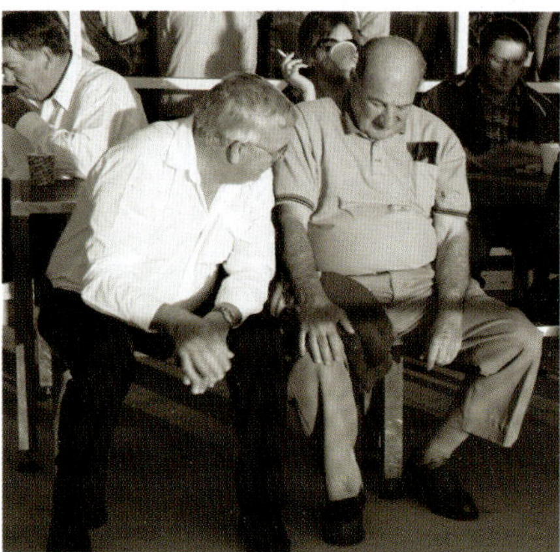

The Monochrome setting discards colour information when it is used for shooting JPEGs.

adjustments is that the adjusted settings are locked into the image file (unless you shoot raw files). The adjustment range is also somewhat limited, compared with the adjustments available in image editing software – including raw file converters. For this reason, we advise photographers to use these in-camera controls judiciously.

It is usually better to make most of these adjustments on your personal computer. The computer's processing system is much more powerful than your camera's microprocessor. Your monitor is also much larger and more colour accurate so it's easier to be discerning when tweaking image files. Finally, if you don't like the changes you have made, it's easy to go back to your original (unadjusted) image and start again.

CUSTOM FUNCTIONS

Further extending the ability for photographers to customise their cameras, almost all DSLRs include one or more Custom memory banks where a large number of pre-determined camera settings are stored. Settings in these memory banks let you choose from a range of options or make selective adjustments to a particular control or shooting parameter. A typical entry-level DSLR may have as many as 20 separate settings that are controllable through the Custom Function, while a professional DSLR will have 60 or more.

Parameters that can be adjusted in the Custom Function menu include allocating particular button controls to adjust settings like image size and quality, exposure compensation, image tone pre-set, exposure or flash adjustment, autofocus mode, or AF point selection. The Custom Function menu can also be used to switch noise reduction on and off and/or control the level of noise reduction processing.

Other Custom Functions may include controlling the flash synchronisation speed, AE and AF lock functions, AF assist beam, flash metering, shutter curtain synchronisation for flash shots and exposure level increments (1/3, ½ or 1EV steps). Mechanical controls like mirror lock-up (for sensor cleaning or very long exposures), are usually covered in the Custom Function menu as well, along with power management and LCD display settings.

Some cameras also include bracketing settings for exposure, focusing and white balance in the Custom Function menu. Extension of the ISO sensitivity range may also be provided. Other cameras provide controls for matching the image sensor and processing

COLOUR SPACE SETTINGS

The colour space setting on a digital camera delineates the range of colours it can reproduce. The default setting on all digital cameras is sRGB, which covers the colours that can be displayed on a computer or TV monitor. Most enthusiast and all professional DSLRs offer an additional colour space setting, known as Adobe RGB, which can record a wider range of hues and tones (see diagram).

Landscape photographers who plan to print their best shots usually find the Adobe RGB setting gives them more colour information to work with and produces prints with a wider colour and tonal range. It's also suitable for photographers who like to shoot raw files and edit them before making prints. However, it's less relevant for portraiture and images captured with this colour space setting may look a little flat on many computer monitors. Many entry-level and multi-function printers can't reproduce all the Adobe RGB tones.

The default sRGB colour space setting will generally give the best results for most normal photography, especially shots of people. It should also be used for shots that are destined for online applications (emails and websites) and photos that will be displayed on a TV screen.

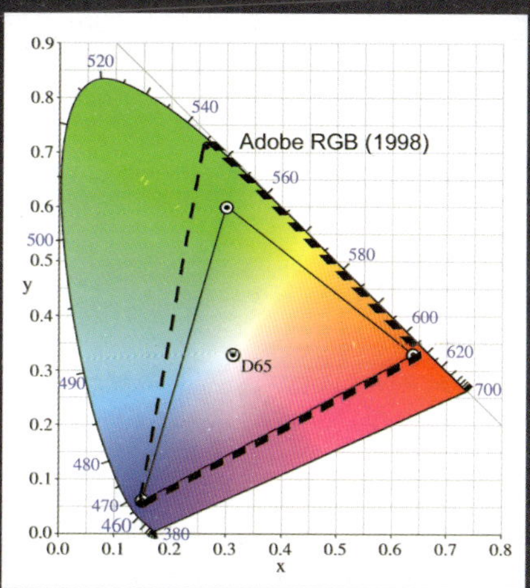

control to a selected lens. For professional DSLRs that accept interchangeable focusing screens, the correct Custom Function must be set to match the exposure correction to the screen in use.

It is worth reading through your camera's instruction manual to see which functions can be adjusted through the Custom Function menu. Check the default settings to ensure the camera is adjusted to meet your own requirements before you embark on a shoot.

✱ USEFUL URLS

The following websites provide additional information on the topics covered in this chapter.

en.wikipedia.org/wiki/Shutter_speed provides useful general information on shutter speeds.

en.wikipedia.org/wiki/F-number provides complementary information on lens apertures.

web.canon.jp/imaging/enjoydslr/index.html is an online tutorial covering shooting with a DSLR camera.

■ ↗ **www.photoreview.com.au/guides for direct links..**

CHAPTER 7

ISO and White Balance

Photographers who are changing from film to digital capture will encounter a couple of new controls that handle recording functions that were formerly dictated by your choice of film: sensitivity and colour balance. One of the benefits of a digital camera is the ability to change these parameters on a shot-by-shot basis, instead of being committed to the film's pre-set values. Fortunately, both settings are easily understood and simple to relate to similar aspects of film choice.

SENSITIVITY

Just as film sensitivity was dictated by the ISO rating of the film, the ISO setting on a digital camera adjusts the sensor's sensitivity to light. The higher the ISO number, the more light-sensitive the sensor is forced to become. Most modern sensors have been designed to work best at ISO settings around 100, so the output signal from the sensor must be boosted to reach higher ISO settings.

When the signal from the sensor is boosted, any image noise (random disruption to the stability of the digital signal) in the digital signal is also increased. The resulting 'noise' will often be visible in your pictures. (See Chapter 2 for more information on image noise.)

The potential for image noise to affect picture quality is directly related to the size of the camera's image sensor. Larger sensors with bigger photosites can collect more light and are, therefore, much less susceptible to image noise than small sensors.

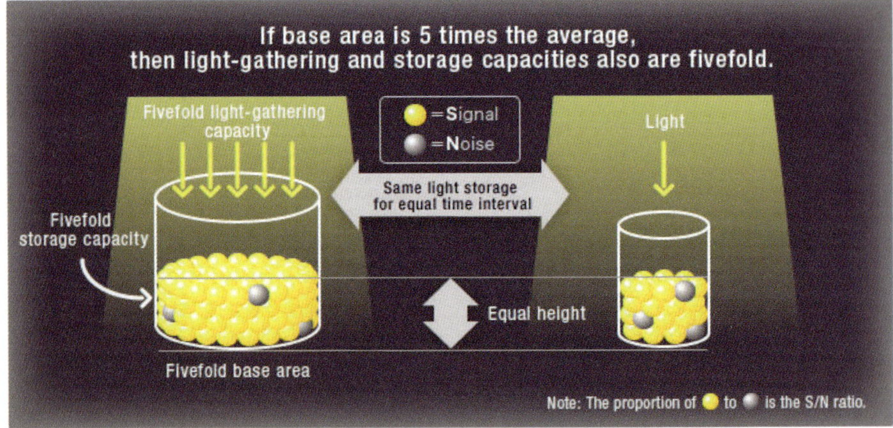

If you envisage each photosite as a bucket that collects light, the large photosite on the left collects many more photons of light (yellow balls) than the small photosite on the right. However, the amount of random noise (grey balls) is the same for both photosites. Consequently, the signal-to-noise ratio is much better for the larger photosite – and this translates to better picture quality. (Picture supplied by Canon.)

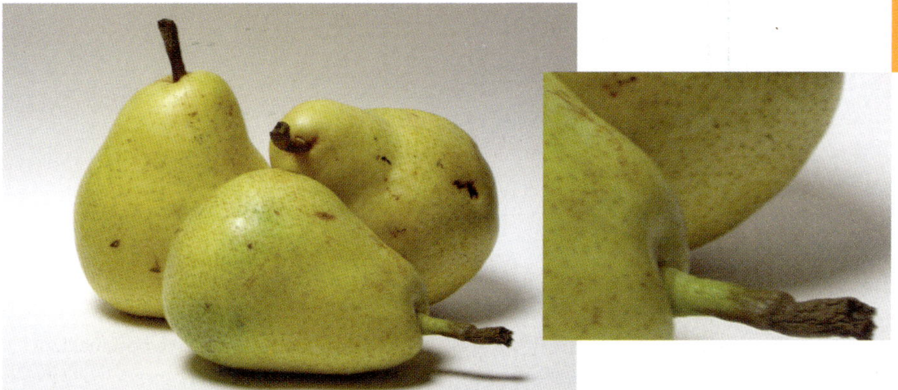

The image above was photographed at ISO 100. The cropped enlargement shows the very low noise levels typical of this sensitivity setting.

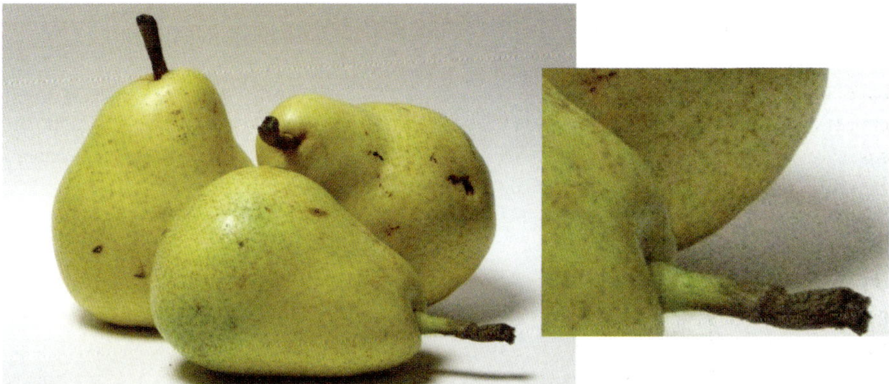

The same subject photographed at ISO 1600. Note the evidence of image noise in the cropped enlargement.

Fortunately, when you use a modern DSLR camera, noise is seldom visible unless you shoot with ISO settings above 400 – and then, it may only be seen when the image is enlarged substantially. Even shots taken at ISO 1600 can produce acceptable A3-sized prints when they have been captured with a DSLR camera. In contrast, noise is often visible at ISO 400 in shots taken with compact digicams and shots taken at ISO 1600 may be unprintable at snapshot size.

USING HIGH ISO SETTINGS

All modern DSLR cameras provide a range of ISO settings from ISO 200 to ISO 1600 and many extend that range down to ISO 100 and up to ISO 3200 – or higher. DSLR cameras vary widely in the range of ISO adjustments they permit. Some will only allow users to select from a pre-set range that is usually between ISO 100 and ISO 1600. Some professional DSLRs support ISO settings up to 25,600, although such high settings are only accessible through a dedicated Custom Function.

Entry-level and 'pro-sumer' DSLRs also include an Auto ISO setting, which allows the camera to determine the optimum ISO setting for the subject. In many cases, photographers can set an upper limit to the Auto ISO range, either in the main camera menu or as a Custom Function. Many DSLRs allow photographers to adjust ISO settings in 1/2 or 1/3 step increments. This choice is usually provided in the Custom Function menu.

In practice, you need to balance shooting convenience against potential for noise when adjusting ISO settings. Choose a low ISO for the majority of shots – including long exposures. But be prepared to increase the camera's sensitivity when conditions demand it, taking into account the potential for noise in the resulting shot.

Be conscious of the effect temperature can have on image noise at ISO settings of 800 and above and be cautious about using the top ISO values when the temperature is above about 15 degrees Celsius. Noise can become particularly obvious when high ISO settings are combined with long exposures at temperatures of 20 degrees Celsius and above.

WHITE BALANCE

The white balance setting is used to make the colours in a digital photograph look natural under a variety of lighting conditions. It works by balancing the colour data from the camera's red, green and blue (RGB) channels. These primary colours are found in all light sources in varying proportions, depending on the 'colour temperature' of the light source. With a high colour temperature, the light has more blue; with a low colour temperature it's redder.

Although you may not notice these colour casts when framing a shot, your digital camera's sensor will record them. Fortunately, the white balance control on the camera allows you to compensate for any colour imbalances in the light that illuminates the subject.

All digital cameras include an auto white

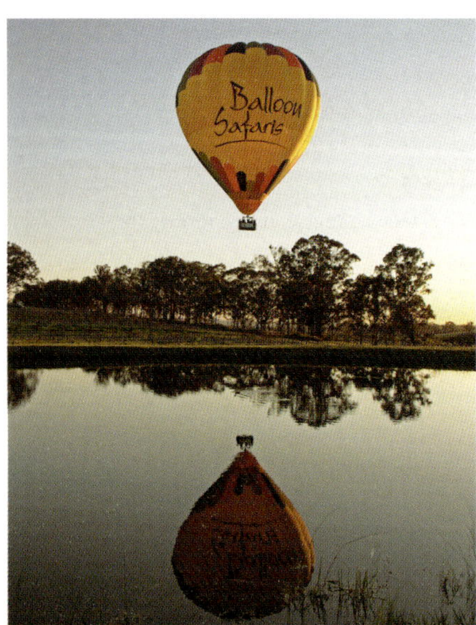

Use low ISO settings for the majority of shots to minimise the effect of noise.(Taken with ISO 100 sensitivity, 1/20 second at f/9.9.)

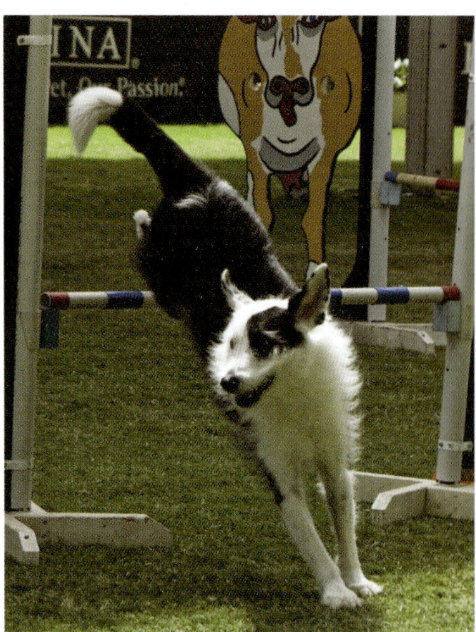

High ISO settings are useful for capturing fast action in poorly- or unevenly-lit situations. (Taken with ISO 800 sensitivity, 1/800 second at f/6.3.)

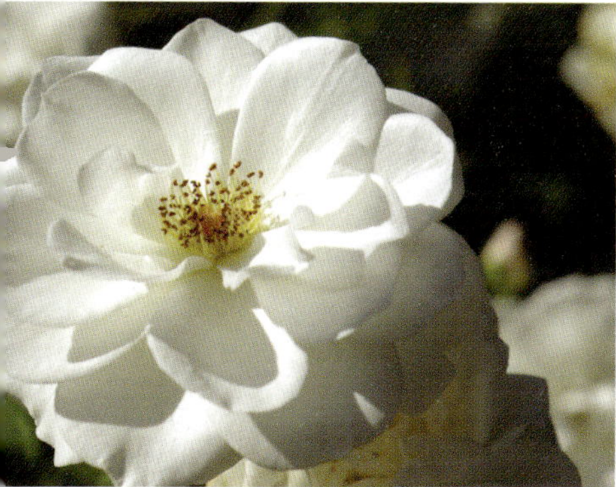

The auto white balance should be able to produce a natural colour balance under a wide range of lighting conditions. (Compare the colours in this image with the colours produced by other white balance settings on this and the next page.)

balance (AWB) setting that evaluates the light reaching the sensor and adjusts the colour balance to correct for colour shifts. The performance of these AWB controls ranges from very effective to relatively poor, with most having some difficulty removing the orange cast caused by incandescent lighting, although they usually perform well with fluorescent lighting.

All DSLRs include a range of white balance pre-sets that cover common lighting conditions like incandescent ('tungsten'), daylight, shade, cloudy, flash and fluorescent (up to three settings in some cameras).

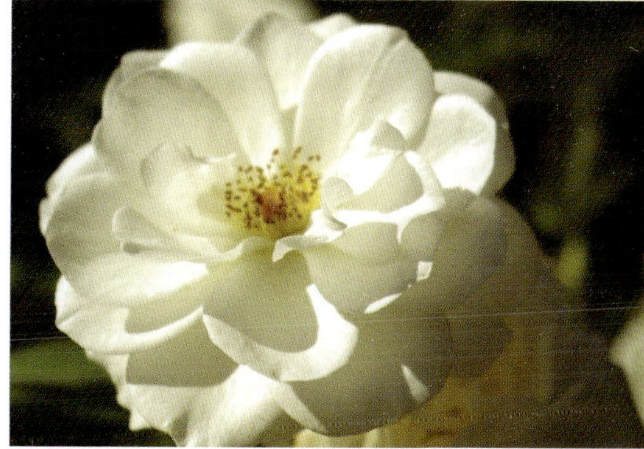

The **Cloudy** setting adds yellow and red.

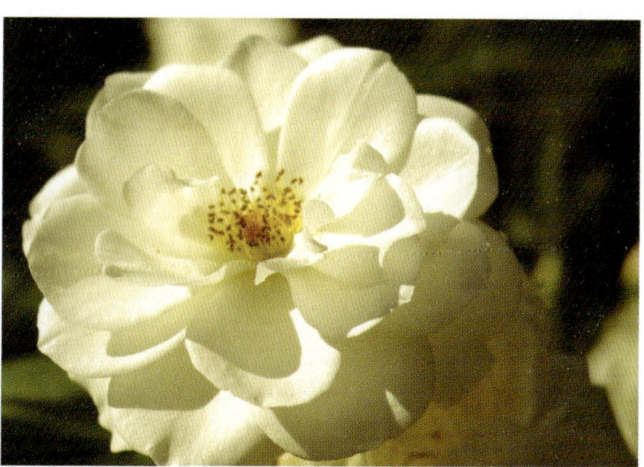

The **Shade** setting is even warmer.

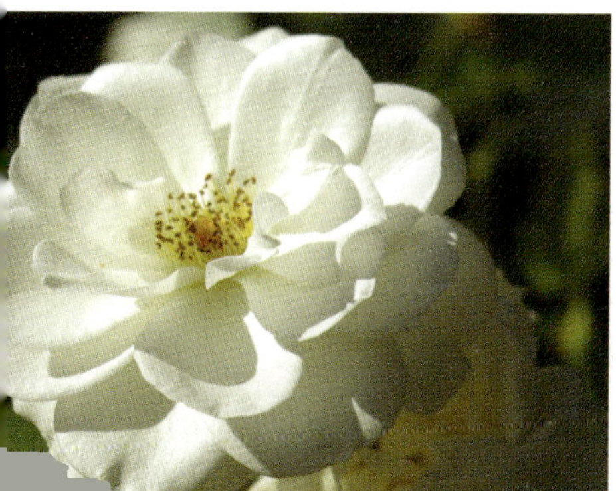

The **Daylight** setting adds a touch of yellow to counteract the blue of the sky.

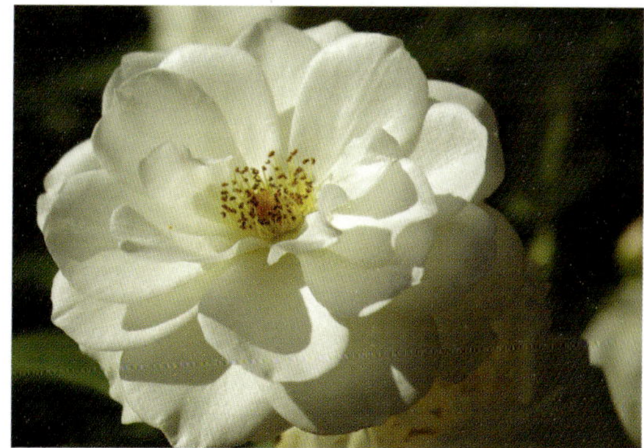

The **Flash** setting adds slightly less yellow than the Daylight setting because the blue bias in electronic flash light is not as strong.

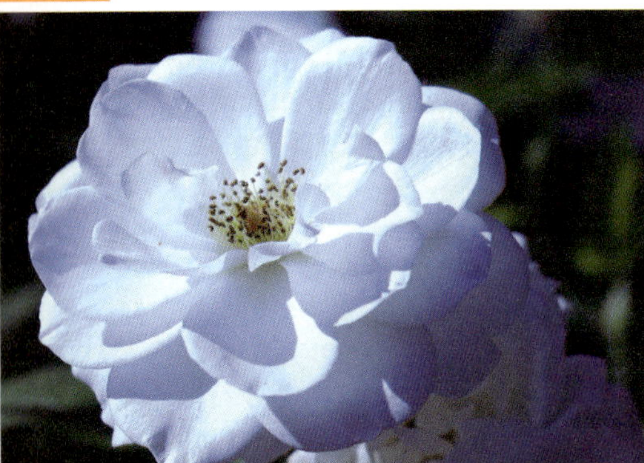

The Incandescent light setting is strongly blue to counteract the red/orange cast of household tungsten lighting.

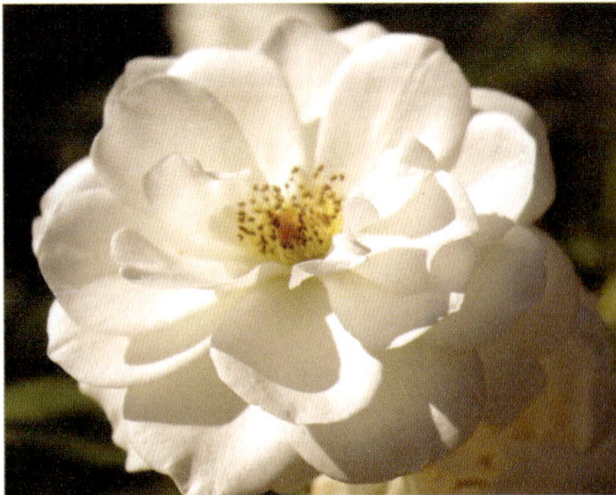

The Cool White Fluorescent setting adds yellow and magenta to counteract the green cast of some fluorescent tubes.

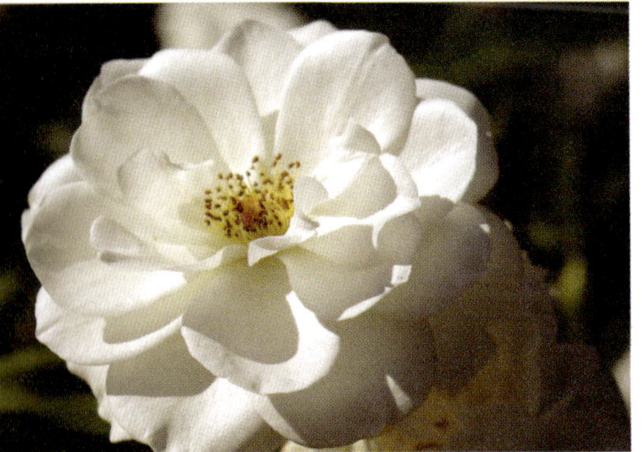

The Daylight Fluorescent setting adds a hint of magenta.

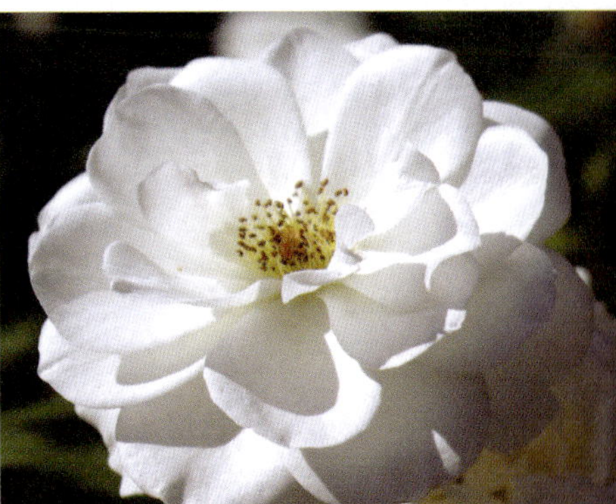

The Warm White Fluorescent setting adds a touch of blue.

Many cameras also provide a manual or 'custom' setting, which is denoted by the following symbol: This setting lets you measure the colour of the illuminating light and use the result to remove unwanted colour casts. The process is straightforward. Simply cover the subject with a plain white object (sheet of paper or white card) and set the lens focus to manual before taking an exposure or white balance reading to capture the colour of the illuminating light. (Some cameras can record the light without taking the shot.)

Some cameras require you to set the white balance to Custom or Manual and select the captured image. For others, this process takes place automatically. The recorded white balance data is used to correct the colour balance in the subsequent shot.

Success depends on getting the initial exposure (which captures the colour data) right. If it's either over- or under-exposed, subsequent shots may be off-colour. Some cameras alert photographers when this happens – but most don't so you should always check your shots when using this strategy.

Most DSLR cameras allow photographers to fine-tune white balance settings along the blue/amber and magenta/green colour bands. Up to nine levels of adjustment are usually provided, enabling users to remove most residual colour casts.

Many also include white balance bracketing, which takes three shots, varying the colour tone from one to the next. Depending on the selected WB mode, the bracketing will be biased to magenta/green or blue/amber. In most cases up to three steps of adjustment in each direction is available. White balance bracketing is useful in mixed lighting when it is difficult for the camera's auto or pre-set system to produce accurate colour reproduction.

In most pro-sumer and professional cameras, photographers can set white balance relative to the Kelvin colour temperature scale. This can be a huge time saver when shooting with professional lighting as all studio lights are standardised to specific Kelvin values and you can simply dial in a correction to match the lights you use. The table on the right shows the Kelvin temperatures for some frequently-used lighting types.

Some factors in this table deserve attention. Note that most types of lighting involve a range of Kelvin values. Only standardised lighting types (studio lights and daylight) have single values.

Type of Light Source	Kelvin Temperature
Sunrise or sunset	2000-3000K
Household incandescent bulbs	2500-2900K
Photographic tungsten lighting	3000K
Halogen lights	3200-3500K
Fluorescent lights	3200-7500K
Mid-afternoon sunlight	4500-5000K
Average noon daylight	5500K
Sun through clouds or haze	5800-6500K
Overcast sky	6000-7500K
Open shade	6500-8000K
Clear blue sky (without direct sun)	10,000-16,000K

Note also the wider range of Kelvin values for fluorescent lighting, due to the different types of fluorescent tubes on sale: daylight, warm white and cool white being the most common. Fluorescent lighting is also 'spiky', with stronger emissions in specific colour bands. This can make correction of colour casts tricky, although (perhaps surprisingly) most cameras' auto and pre-set modes come pretty close to accurate colour reproduction.

The colour bias of a clear blue sky or open shade can be influenced by the latitude where the photograph is taken. Kelvin values are usually higher for these situations at higher latitudes. Consequently, some degree of fine-tuning may be required for most lighting types. ■

✱ USEFUL URLS

The following websites provide additional information on the topics covered in this chapter.

en.wikipedia.org/wiki/Film_speed contains an interesting history of the use of ISO settings from the days of film to digital photography.

en.wikipedia.org/wiki/White_balance provides a good overview of white balance.

↗ **www.photoreview.com.au/guides for direct links.**

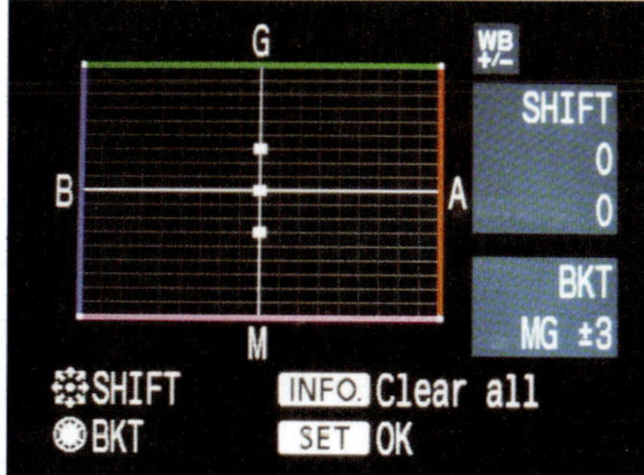

Many DSLR cameras include controls for tuning white balance settings. Adjustments can be made on two colour axes: blue/amber and green/magenta.

CHAPTER 8

File Formats

Despite several attempts to replace it over the past decade, JPEG (pronounced Jay Peg) remains the universal file format for digital imaging. Not only is it used by all digital cameras (including camcorders and cameraphones) for image capture, it's also the universal file format for sharing digital pictures online, both in websites and via emails. JPEG files can also be displayed on all computer monitors and most TV sets and printed by all photo printers. Virtually any software application that can handle digital images is JPEG compatible.

Two other file formats are also offered in DSLR cameras: raw and TIFF (Tagged image File Format), although the latter is becoming increasingly rare. Each of these has its own advantages and, although the default setting in all DSLRs is for JPEG capture, there may be times when one of the other file formats is a better option. In this chapter we'll look at the advantages and disadvantages of the three most popular file formats and consider why digital photographers should consider other file formats.

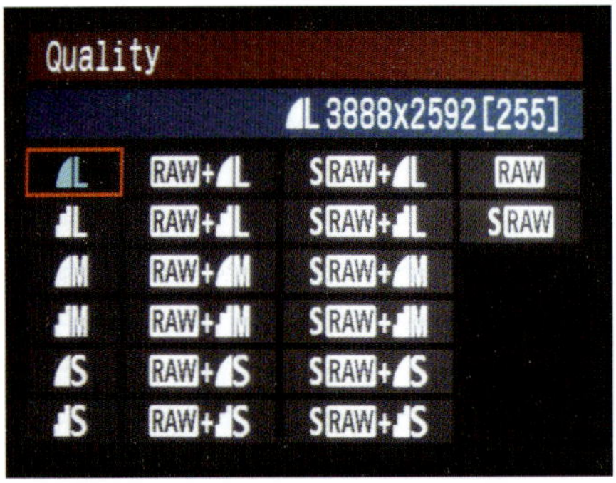

HOW CAMERAS RECORD JPEGS

When you capture JPEG files, the camera's microprocessor converts the raw image data into RGB pixel values (a process known as demosaicing) then applies white balance, saturation, sharpening and other adjustments according to pre-determined formulae. These settings are effectively locked into the image file. The camera's on-board microprocessor then compresses the image and down-samples it from 12 bits of information per pixel (which is captured by the camera) to 8 bits.

JPEG compression works by dividing the image into small blocks and discarding data that is unlikely to be missed by the human eye. And this is the main downside of the JPEG format: image data is lost. The more the image is compressed (by adjusting the Quality setting), the more information is discarded. This 'lost' data can never be recovered; hence JPEG is a 'lossy' file format.

The actual size of a JPEG file depends on the complexity of the subject that has been photographed. Shots containing large areas of blue sky can tolerate a higher degree of compression so they can be two to three times smaller than pictures of detailed subjects – even though they might have originally been the same size as uncompressed files.

One of the advantages of the JPEG format is that the degree of compression is easily

More sophisticated DSLR cameras provide a wide range of file size and compression level choices. Recent cameras have added a 'small RAW' (sRAW) format, which records raw files with a smaller image size.

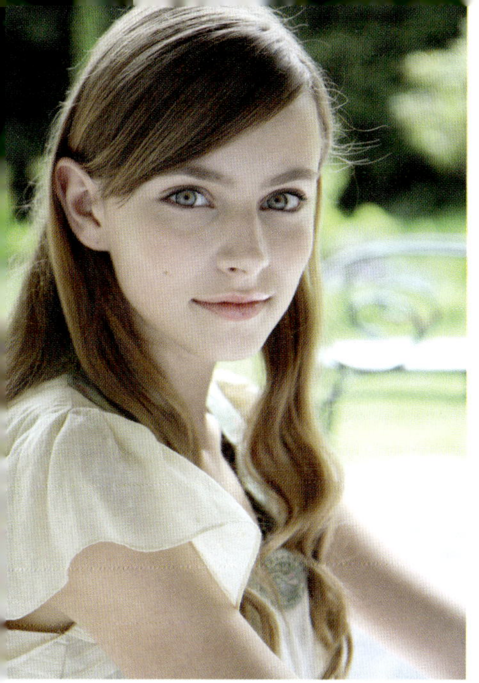

A typical digital photograph, captured in JPEG format. (Source: Canon.)

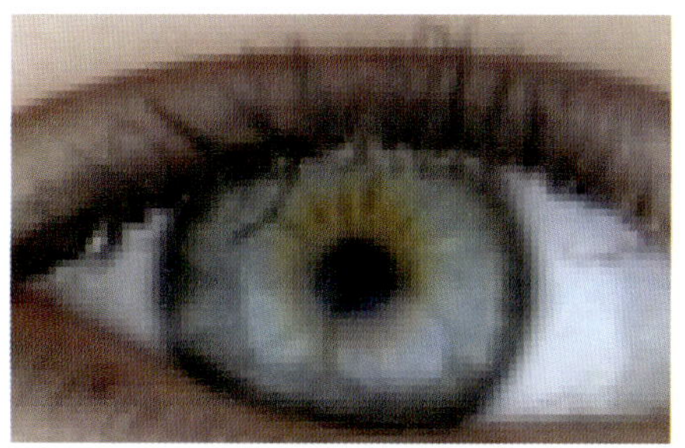

Progressive enlargements of a small section containing detail shows the blocky structure that results from JPEG compression. (The image on the top is a 1095 x 789 pixel, 274-kilobyte file while the enlargement on the bottom is a 1093 x 790 pixel, 206-kilobyte file.)

If we take a similar-sized enlargement from part of the image with little detail, the file size is reduced to 120 kilobytes, showing the influence the amount of detail has on JPEG file sizes.

adjustable. Almost all digital cameras provide at least two compression levels in the image 'Quality' setting; typically designated 'Fine' and 'Normal'. The image 'Size' setting has nothing to do with the JPEG format. It simply determines the size of the pixel array that makes up the image. It, too, is adjustable in most cameras.

WHEN TO SHOOT JPEGS

Novice photographers – and photographers who have no interest in editing their digital photographs – should generally leave their cameras set to capture JPEGs. However, to take advantage of the high resolution and quality of the camera's sensor and image processing system it is pointless to shoot with anything other than the cameras highest resolution and quality settings.

Always shoot with the image size on Large and the quality setting on Fine (or Super-Fine if the camera offers it) It's easy to reduce the size of image files post-capture if you want to send them in emails or post them on the Web. However, it is impossible to put back image data that wasn't recorded in the first place because

DIGITAL SLR POCKET GUIDE

the camera was set on Small size and Normal (or Basic) compression.

JPEGs are the best starting point for images that are destined exclusively for use on websites and in emails as other types of image files must be converted to JPEGs before they can be posted online. Many panorama stitching programs can only be used with JPEGs. It is also unlikely that anybody could see much difference between images shot as JPEGs and those captured in other file formats unless the shots covered an extended brightness range and/or unless they were enlarged considerably.

RAW FILES

Raw files contain the image data as it is captured by the camera's sensor with only minimal processing applied. Many photographers liken them to 'digital negatives' because they must be processed on a computer using special software to yield optimal results. They're quite different from JPEG images and have significant advantages for serious photographers.

When you shoot raw files, all of the information recorded by each photosite is used by the camera's image processor to create the digital image. Nothing is discarded, even when the image processor compresses the raw file to make it smaller. The compression is 'lossless' which means all of the image data is retained – and usable by the photographer for subsequent editing.

All raw files require subsequent editing so, unless you are prepared to edit your digital images, there is no point in shooting raw files. Editing raw files is a two-stage process. The files must first be converted into an editable format (either JPEG or TIFF). They can then be fine-tuned with image editing software for subsequent printing. (See Chapter 11 for more information on this topic.)

A good raw file converter will integrate effectively with your workflow - and your favourite editing software. This integration should include

BIT DEPTH

A bit is the smallest unit of measurement for digital data. Bit depth refers to the number of colours that can be displayed by a digital device. The higher the bit depth, the more colours used in the image and, consequently, the larger the file size.

JPEG images are always recorded with 8-bit depth. This means the files can record 256 (28) levels of red, green and blue. Cameras that support raw file capture offer higher bit depths, usually ranging from 12 to16 bits. A 12-bit image file can record 4096 levels of each of the three colour channels, while a 16-bit image file can cover 65,536 discrete levels of red, green and blue information.

The main reason bit depth is important to digital photographers is that images with higher bit depth give you so much more data to work with when the image is edited than 8-bit JPEGs. Consequently, you can make a wider range of adjustments without compromising picture quality. If you don't plan to edit your digital photos and print them to poster size, the ability to work with high-bit images is irrelevant; you might just as well stick with JPEG files.

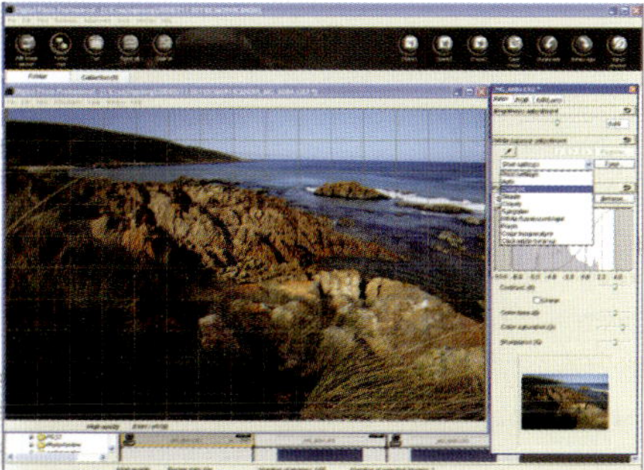

An effective raw file processor provides a full set of parameter adjustments and integrates well with your image editing software.

a raw file browser and the ability to apply settings from one image to a group of other images.

RAW FILE ADVANTAGES

In contrast to JPEGS, raw files are information-rich. Each raw file will contain the maximum bit depth the camera can record. In effect, this gives you at least three times the amount of digital information that is recorded in a JPEG file – and three times the latitude for making adjustments to brightness, contrast and colour levels before any processing artefacts become visible.

You can correct errors in exposure, adjust brightness levels to ensure both highlights and shadows contain detail, remove colour casts and, generally, make your digital photograph look as much like the original scene you photographed without losing any of the fine tonal nuances that make the difference between an excellent digital picture and a poor one.

Shooting raw files allows you to take control of the white balance, saturation, sharpening and contrast adjustments during the conversion process. And, because it is done on your own computer, you have much more processing power at your fingertips than the camera can

possibly provide.

Most raw converters allow you to recover highlight detail in images that have been overexposed by up to one stop. In contrast, there's not much you can do with an overexposed JPEG image. If no highlight detail was captured, no amount of editing can bring it back. In the case of under-exposure, most raw converters provide a similar latitude for detail recovery and the resulting image should not be excessively noise affected. In contrast, recovering shadow detail from an under-exposed JPEG usually results in visible shadow noise.

Finally, you can output the image as a 16-bit TIFF file, which gives you a robust platform for further editing.

RAW FILE DISADVANTAGES

The main problem with raw files is that they are proprietary. Not only is Canon's format different from Nikon's, Olympus's and Sony's and everyone else's, but raw formats may also vary from model to model within a manufacturer's range. Consequently, photographers who plan to shoot raw files must make sure any raw conversion software or image-editing application they buy supports the raw images from the camera(s) they plan to use.

All cameras that support raw file capture are supplied with a software disk containing software for converting raw files into JPEG or TIFF files. The capabilities of the software bundle vary widely between different manufacturers. Some provide a wider range of adjustments than others and some have more intuitive user interfaces. Some include basic editing software, while others don't.

Raw files are also relatively large. For a 10-megapixel camera, file sizes range from

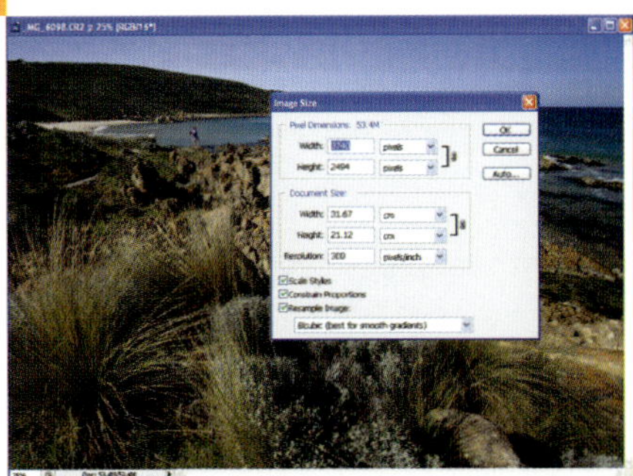

Raw files are very large, relative to JPEG files. This 3740 x 2494 pixel image has a file size of 53.4 megabytes, compared with 4.98 megabytes for the JPEG file of the same shot.

approximately 9MB to 30MB (depending on the amount of detail in the shot and the degree of compression the camera applies), compared with 3MB to 5MB for a high-quality JPEG. This means you can store fewer images on a card and it will usually take longer to transfer image files to your computer. It may also reduce the continuous shooting capacity of your camera as the buffer memory will fill up sooner.

Having to convert your images from raw to an editable format (JPEG or TIFF) adds an extra step to your workflow. If this is irksome to you, you're probably better off shooting JPEGs – especially if you don't print your shots any larger than A4 size. ∎

✳ USEFUL URLS

The following websites provide additional information on the topics covered in this chapter.

www.photoreview.com.au/ contains several articles on file formats.

en.wikipedia.org/wiki/Graphics_file_format provides an overview of file formats plus information on image file compression.

www.adobe.com/products/dng/ has information on the 'universal' Digital Negative raw file format and its advantages to photographers.

www.luminous-landscape.com/tutorials/bit-depth.shtml has an easy-to-understand tutorial on bit depth and its relevance to DSLR photography.

↗ **www.photoreview.com.au/guides for direct links.**

TIFF FILES

Even if your camera doesn't include TIFF as a capture option, you will probably convert your raw files into TIFF format for subsequent editing. The advantages of the TIFF format are few – but significant:

1. Like raw files, they can contain all the pixel data that makes up the image. This provides much more editing flexibility than JPEGs.
2. Like JPEGs they can be 'read' and manipulated in almost all editing software and printed on almost every printer.

However, TIFF files have a couple of disadvantages. For starters, they are usually very large. A 16-bit TIFF file from a 10-megapixel DSLR camera can contain more than 60MB of image data. This makes them unusable in web-based situations and too large to send via emails. TIFF files also contain adjustments applied by the image processing system in the camera (in the case of cameras that include TIFF capture) or in the editing software. These adjustments may not be appropriate for your requirements and will, therefore, need to be over-ridden, which can compromise picture quality.

CHAPTER 9

Live Viewing

Many of the latest DSLR cameras allow photographers to compose shots using the LCD monitor on the camera as well as the normal viewfinder. This Live View mode makes them as easy to use as a digicam and is one of the more attractive features novice photographers look for. However, live viewing has some significant benefits for experienced photographers as well.

It's particularly valuable in situations where it is difficult to look through the viewfinder to compose shots, such as in crowd scenes where the camera must be held above your head or for taking close-ups of objects close to the ground and achieving precise compositions for macro and technical shots. It also comes in handy for portrait photographers because it allows them to engage with subjects without having the barrier of a camera between them.

The ability to see the subject exactly as the camera's sensor 'sees' it is another benefit because it allows you to check focusing, exposure levels and colour balance in real-time and see the result you should obtain. Live View Is great for checking image stabilisation.

It's also an asset when you shoot with a remote control as well as for people who wear glasses. Live viewing is particularly useful for underwater photographers because it provides a view that is easy to see through a diving mask when the camera is in a waterproof housing.

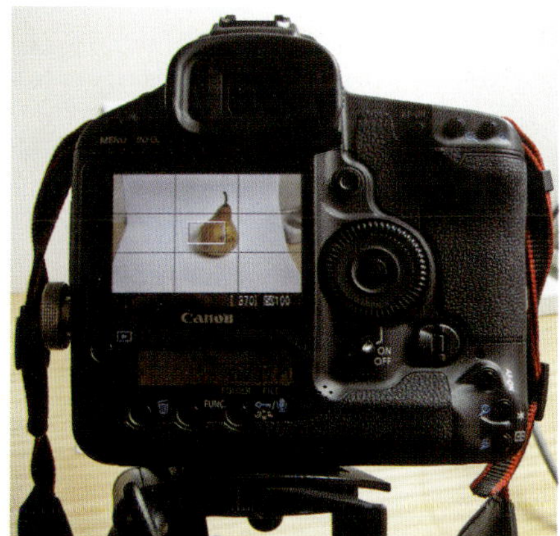

The Live View mode allows photographers to compose shots on the camera's LCD screen, just as they can with a digicam. Grid overlays can be superimposed to assist shot composition.

Live View mode is usually engaged via the camera's menu system. Some Live View settings are controlled through the Custom Menu settings.

The main downside of live viewing is that it tends to be somewhat slower to use than viewfinder-based shooting. Because several components in the mirror mechanism must be moved to provide the live view, it usually takes longer to capture the shot. For this reason, Live View is best used for stationary subjects and really excels for studio photography.

Live viewing also involves higher power consumption. Because the sensor must remain active while the Live View mode is in use, the number of shots per charge decreases between 20% and 40%. Photographers must also keep a check on the camera's working temperature as overheating can damage circuitry in high ambient temperatures. Most Live View systems shut down after a short time to prevent overheating.

LIVE VIEW TYPES

The first Live View function introduced in a DSLR camera used a separate sensor to provide the live view display. This strategy is still in use in some DSLRs because it allows the lens to be focused without raising the main reflex mirror. Focusing is measurably faster with this type of Live View.

More recent applications of live viewing tend to favour using the camera's image sensor to provide the live view for the LCD screen. This technique has the advantage of showing photographers the exact view the sensor will record; in other words 100% coverage of the subject.

When Live View mode is selected, half-pressing the shutter button flips the mirror up, blocking off the viewfinder. The image 'seen' by the camera's sensor can be displayed on the LCD monitor. Most cameras allow you to simulate an exposure and/or zoom in to check the focus and fine detail in the shot. Many also allow you to enlarge the preview image to check focusing.

The other system blocks off the viewfinder and directs the light path to a secondary sensor, usually in the viewfinder housing, which provides the image for the LCD. This means there's no need for the mirror to be raised to provide the live view. At the same time, the semi-reflecting main mirror passes light down to the AF sensor below the mirror chamber in the normal manner.

This allows the TTL phase-detection AF system to function normally in Live View mode, without requiring a separate contrast-detect AF system. The dual sensor design allows the camera's AF system to be as responsive in Live View mode as it is when the viewfinder is used for shot composition, which means capture lag is reduced and faster continuous shooting speeds may be supported.

Some DSLRs include a Remote Live View function, which is enabled with special software and outputs the live view as video for viewing on computer monitor. This function improves remote shooting by making it possible to check such things as composition, focus, moiré, and false colours quickly and easily on a monitor screen. It can work in tandem with remote capture systems supported by the camera.

A few cameras can capture a digital preview of the subject in Live View mode. This preview can be saved in JPEG format with the resolution you have selected in the camera's menu.

FOCUSING IN LIVE VIEW MODE

Some cameras that support Live View shooting only support manual focusing, although a few of the more recently-released models allow autofocusing with Live View. Manual focusing is straightforward and involves turning the focusing ring on the lens until the subject looks sharp. Zooming in allows focus checking and you can select a particular AF point to zoom in on so as to be sure the critical areas in the shot are sharp.

Two autofocusing modes are commonly offered in cameras that use the main image

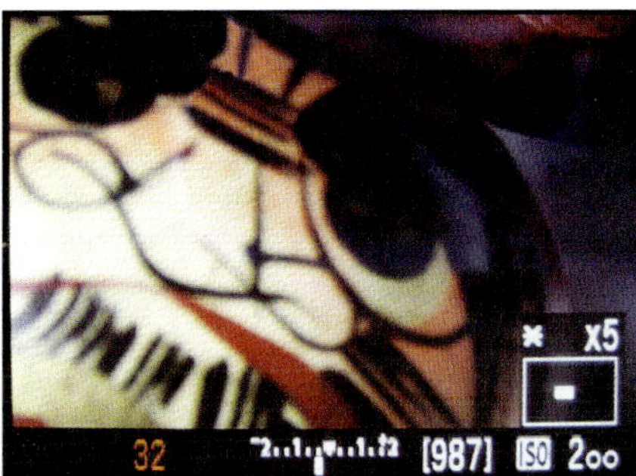

Most DSLRs with Live View shooting capabilities include a magnification function for focus checking. There is no interruption to the live preview when magnification is applied.

sensor for live viewing and support autofocusing. The Quick mode is faster to use than the Live mode. However, the main mirror must be dropped to expose the AF sensor. This temporarily stops the live view and adds a brief delay to the image capture sequence. Most DSLRs in this category use contrast-based autofocusing systems to minimise this delay. However, a few revert to phase difference detection with certain lenses.

The Live mode provides an uninterrupted view of the subject and is used for careful focusing plus exposure verification. Some cameras require you to hold down the AE/AF lock button to engage autofocusing in Live View mode. In a few cameras, this mode also supports 'silent shooting' in which an electronic first-curtain shutter scans silently across the sensor to record the image. It synchronises with the second shutter curtain to provide a slit exposure, thereby controlling light levels.

Cameras with dual-sensor Live View systems may provide a wider range of AF options than the single-sensor cameras. More detailed on-screen image overlays (see below), AF point selection

and more advanced metering sensors may also be provided. However, the second sensor may not show exactly the same view of the subject as the main sensor captures so accurate shot composition may be more difficult to achieve.

If the camera has a depth-of-field preview button, it is usable in Live View mode in some cameras. This function stops the lens down to the shooting aperture and simulates the shooting exposure, enabling a check of metering accuracy in real time.

In some DSLRs, an electronic first-curtain shutter allows the camera to operate in Live View mode with the mechanical shutter completely open. The first curtain of the shutter synchronises with the mechanical second curtain, allowing exposures to be made with a moving slit shutter.

The resulting exposures are silent because the shutter-cocking noise and mirror bounce are eliminated. This system also reduces shutter release lag time and allows the camera to support faster continuous shooting speeds.

IMAGE OVERLAYS IN LIVE VIEW MODE

Pressing the Info or Display button allows you to change the information overlay on the image in Live View mode. Most cameras allow users to toggle between no data displays and varying levels of shooting data. Some will display AF points with or without the exposure metering circle.

Some cameras will also provide a grid line overlay and/or a histogram for checking exposure levels. Selected camera control settings may also be displayed as a semi-transparent overlay on the live view to allow photographers to adjust shooting parameters without leaving Live View. ■

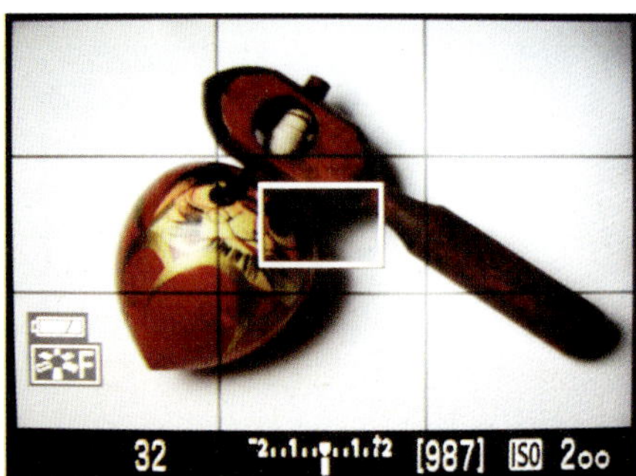

The live preview can be overlaid with a framing grid. The white rectangle in the centre represents the autofocusing sensor. (This can be moved in some cameras.)

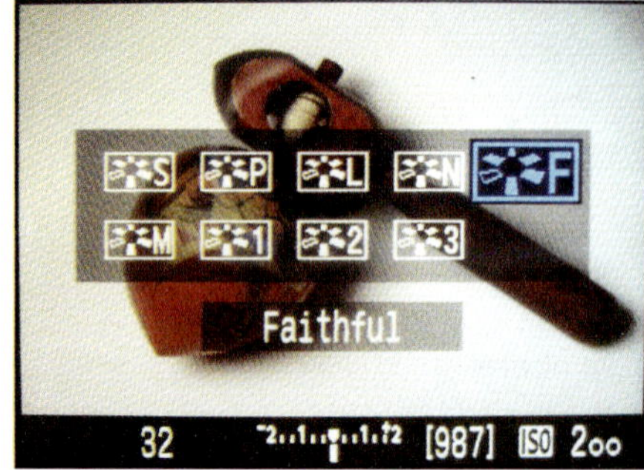

Some other menu settings – in this case the Picture Style menu – can be overlaid on the live preview image.

✳ USEFUL URLS

There are several video clips that demonstrate Live View shooting on You Tube but very few other informative websites covering this topic.

↗ **www.photoreview.com.au/guides for direct links.**

CHAPTER 10

Post-Capture Options

Although all DSLR cameras provide similar basic playback functions to a sophisticated compact digicam, their displays are usually more informative and provide a wider range of shooting data and other information photographers can use to improve their picture-taking. DSLRs will usually provide more options for fine-tuning camera settings, often in special Custom Function menus.

They may also offer better image management facilities and greater control over playback and quick review displays. For example, when captured images are displayed on the camera's monitor after a shot is taken, DSLR photographers can usually determine how long they wish the image to remain on the screen.

Most cameras – both enthusiast and professional - provide the following standard playback options:

1. Playback with magnification. This allows you to magnify part of a displayed image to check focusing and scroll around the image by using the arrow pad keys. A dedicated button is often devoted to this function.

2. Image playback with shooting information, which usually includes the image quality and size settings, the image file number, the date and time the shot was taken, the shutter speed and lens aperture, the ISO and colour space settings, the metering and white balance modes and any corrections or adjustments to parameters like exposure, flash output or white balance.

3. Playback with histogram. All DSLRs provide brightness histograms and many also give

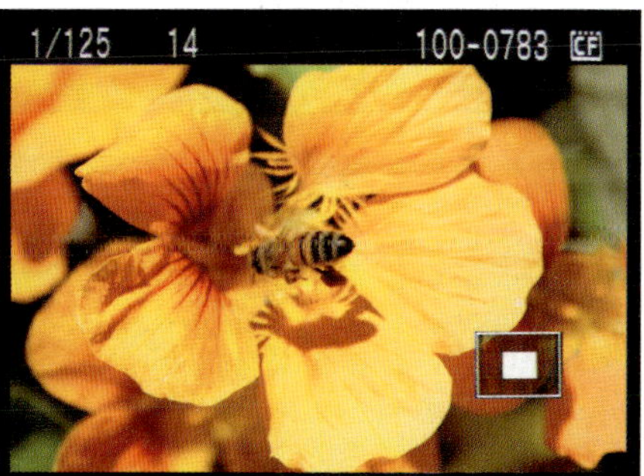

Playback with magnification lets you check the subject is in focus.

separate graphs for the red, green and blue components of the image, making it easy to detect colour casts in the shot.

4. Playback with highlight/shadow alert. In this mode, any over-exposed areas in the subject will blink when highlight alert is selected, while underexposed areas can be made to blink by choosing shadow alert. The degree of over- or underexposure is not shown but photographers can use the EV adjustment control to change exposure settings and then re-take the shot and re-check highlights and shadows once more.

5. Auto rotation of shots taken vertically so they display upright during playback, both on the camera's LCD and when the images are downloaded to a computer. Manual rotation is also supported in most DSLRs.

6. Index displays allow four, nine or 16 shots to be viewed simultaneously on the LCD screen. This function is used for seeing the images already stored on a memory card or locating wanted shots among a large number of files.

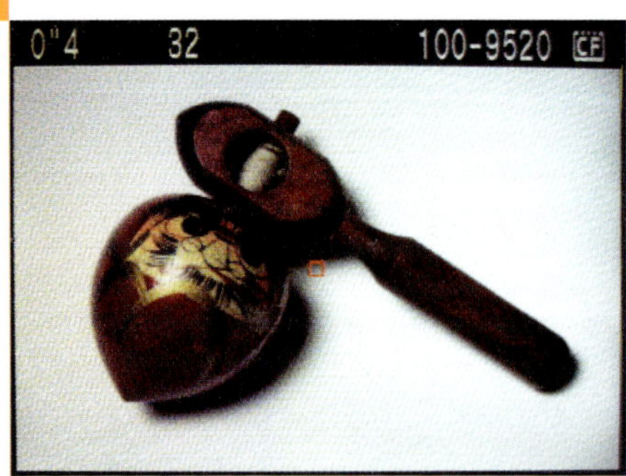
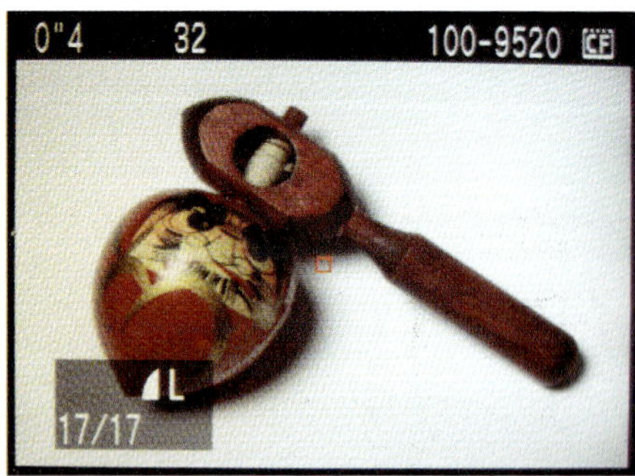
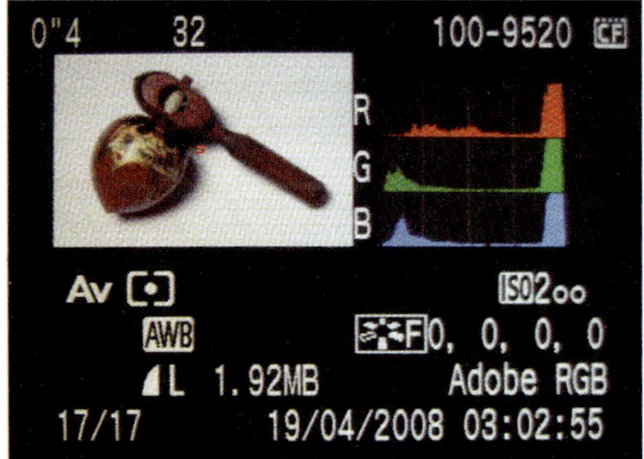
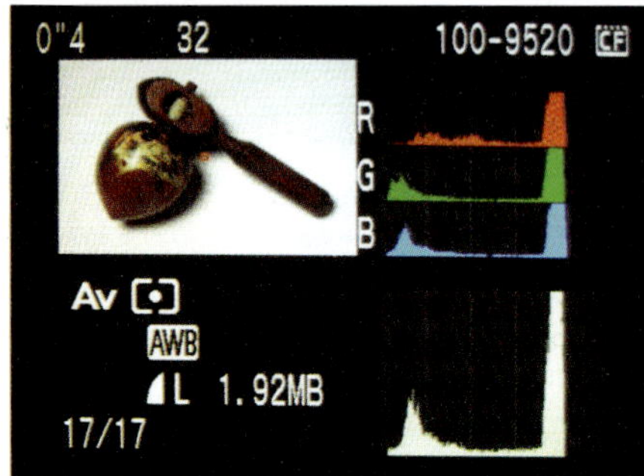

The standard playback options, which are accessed by toggling the Display button. The sequence is as follows: Single image display, Single image plus image-recording quality, Thumbnail plus histogram and shooting data, Thumbnail plus histogram.

To display a single image at full screen size, you select the shot using the arrow pad and press the playback or magnify button.

7. Jump displays, which allow you to jump forward or backward by 10 or 100 images. This option is handy when you have to scroll through a large number of files on a memory card. Some cameras allow the jump function to be used with the magnified view, maintaining a pre-set magnification size and position throughout the jumps.

8. Auto playback as a slide show. Many DSLRs include a slideshow setting that automatically plays back all the shots on a memory card in sequence. Each image is displayed for roughly three seconds.

9. LCD brightness adjustment. Even entry-level DSLRs allow the brightness of the LCD screen to be adjusted. This can make the screen easier to view in normal lighting but may not provide significant improvements in bright sunlight, where all LCDs become difficult to 'read'.

IN-CAMERA FILE MANAGEMENT

All DSLRs include a variety of ways of tracking and organising image files and it's important to understand how they work. Two file numbering methods are common in DSLRs: continuous and auto-reset. Selecting the wrong one can cause images to be over-written and you may lose valuable shots.

Selecting the continuous option ensures the files are numbered in sequence. When you load a new card (or a card from which previously-captured shots have been transferred), the first shot you take is numbered sequentially from the highest file number in the last batch of shots you took. This prevents images from having the

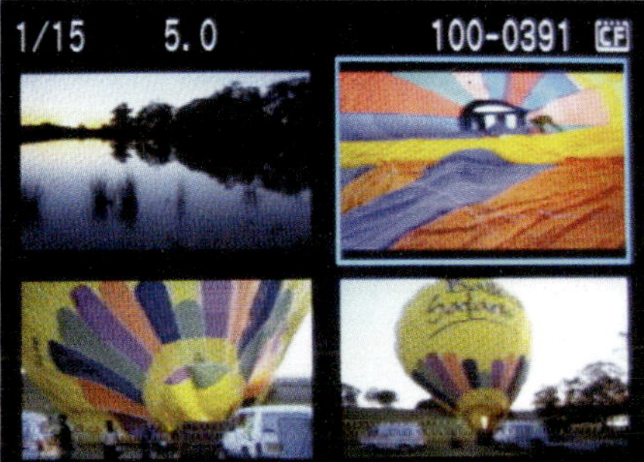

Index displays can show four, nine or 16 frames simultaneously so photographers can see the recent shots they have taken.

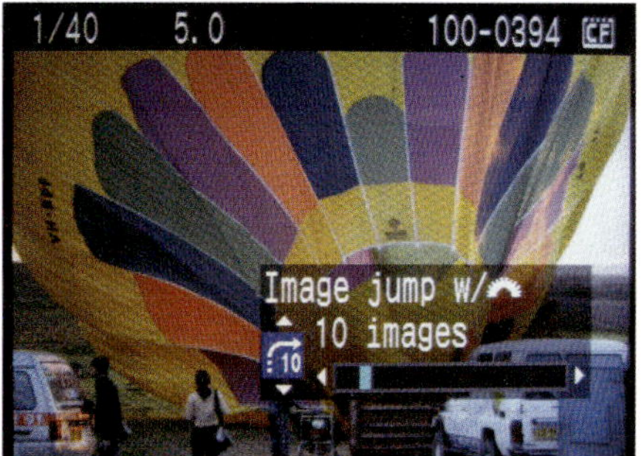

The Jump display lets you scan quickly through a large number of image files on the camera's memory card.

same file number and makes it easier to manage images on your computer.

When the auto-reset function is selected, the camera will automatically start numbering images from the first file number in the folder (e.g. 100-0001) each time you insert a new memory card. In some cameras, earlier files on the card are detected and the file numbering starts from the file with the highest number.

Where image files are likely to be replaced, the camera (or your file downloading program) should warn you and give you the opportunity to download the files to a different folder or change the numbering system. Some applications will do this for you automatically – but the end result can be confusing. The most common result is images from two or more different shooting sessions mixed up together in the same folder on your PC.

Always check the camera's file numbering system before you start using a new DSLR. We recommend using the continuous setting as it makes file management much easier in the long term.

All DSLRs include systems for erasing and protecting image files and tagging shots for automatic printing. The control that erases image files is usually identified by a 'rubbish bin' icon. In most cameras it's a dedicated button, although you may also be able to erase files through the menu system.

Selecting a file for erasure usually calls up a warning screen that checks whether you want to delete the file. The default setting is 'Cancel' so if you wish to trash the file you must select 'OK'. Many cameras allow you to delete all files on a memory card by providing an additional 'delete all files' option. Another way to delete all files is to

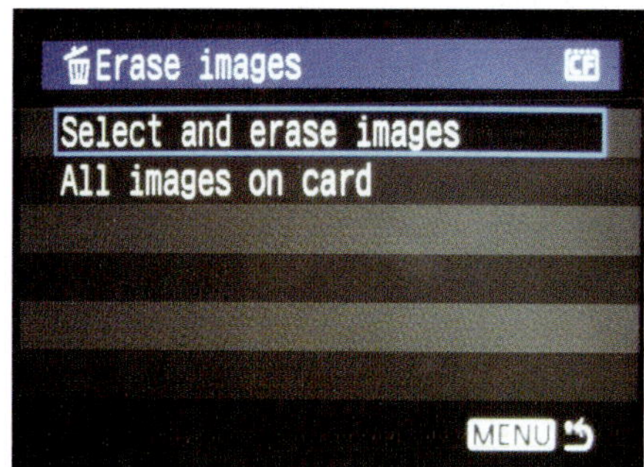

Some cameras provide settings for erasing individual images or selected shots through the menu system.

format the card. This is always done through the camera's menu system.

Deleting individual or tagged files is simple. Select the Delete setting from the playback menu and use the arrow pad to select the displayed file or files. This is not the same as formatting the card.

Tagged files can be readily identified by icons on the thumbnail. For example, protected files are identified by a key icon. Photographers can tag JPEG files (but not raw files) for automatic printing using DPOF (Digital Print Order Format) tags, which can be 'read' by most automatic printers (including photo labs).

The Print Order menu in some cameras can be used to order index prints and imprint the date and/or file number on prints. Note: The print settings are applied to all images tagged for printing so if you tag one image for date and/or file numbering, it will appear on all prints. The memory card must also be the card that was used to capture the shots; you can't download a set of pictures to a spare card and print from them with this function.

DIRECT PRINTING FROM DSLR CAMERAS

Most DSLR cameras support PictBridge direct printing, which was introduced in 2004. When the camera is connected via USB cable to a compatible printer, PictBridge allows users to:

- Print one or more images selected from the camera's monitor display;
- Automatically print images tagged using the DPOF specification;
- Produce an index print of all images;
- Print all images in the camera's memory.

Once again, only JPEG images can be printed via PictBridge (and other proprietary

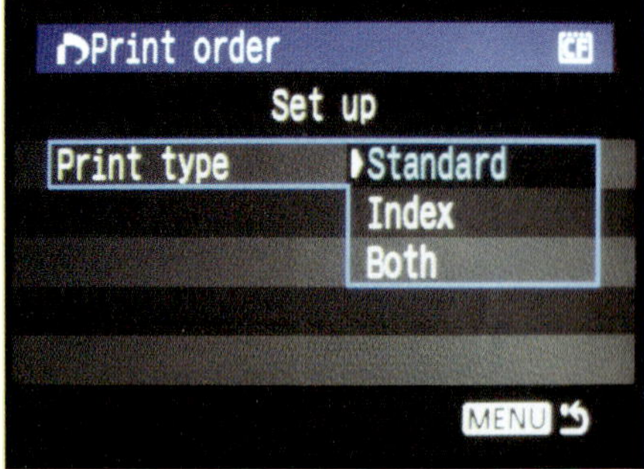

Many DSLRs allow users to tag images for automatic printing, either as single shots or as index prints – or both.

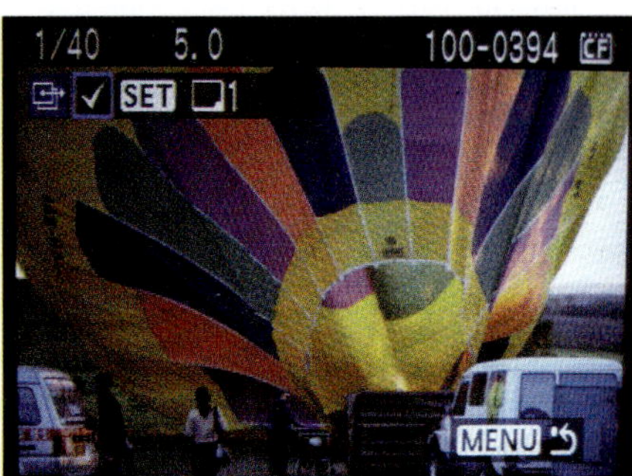

Images that have been tagged for printing are easily identified by a tick mark on the top left corner.

direct printing systems). Direct printing systems have limited value for photographers because they restrict the adjustments you can make to shots before printing. In addition, the only way of viewing the image you want to print is on the camera's monitor, which is usually too small to make accurate assessments of colour and sharpness.

More sophisticated DSLRs include some interesting in-camera controls that allow users to trim shots, adjust brightness, contrast and saturation and convert images to B&W or sepia tone. Red-eye correction for flash shots and dynamic range adjustments may also be provided, along with tilt correction to straighten vertical lines that were distorted by shooting with a wide-angle lens.

DOWNLOADING IMAGE FILES

Image files can be copied to a computer's hard drive by either connecting the camera to the PC via the USB cable supplied with the camera or removing the memory card from the camera and inserting it in a card reader which, itself, is linked to the PC via USB cable. Both work equally well, although downloading via a cable-to-computer link draws power from the camera's battery as the camera must be switched on.

Card readers are convenient if you have several cameras with different types of memory cards or if there are two or more people in a household using the same computer. Turn the camera's power off before removing the memory card.

The software supplied with many cameras includes automatic file management facilities that recognise image files and automatically organise them in folders, which are usually identified with the current date and time. These automatic cataloguers can be convenient but they vary greatly in how well they work. While some are efficient, others can be downright frustrating to use and folders can sometimes be stored in parts of your computer that you may not normally access.

TV CONNECTION

Most DSLRs are supplied with video cables that allow them to be connected to a TV set so you can view the shots on the memory card. The cable plugs into the Video-In terminal on the TV set. Both camera and TV should be switched off when the cables are plugged in.

The camera's video format must be set to match the TV display standard (PAL for Australia for standard definition). A few recently-released cameras support connection to HDTV (high-definition TV) sets, although you may need to purchase the required cable separately. Expect to see this facility becoming more popular as we transition from standard to high-definition TV broadcasting.

Selection of shots for display and moving from one shot to the next is done with the camera's controls, using the playback button and arrow pad. At the end of the show, switch both camera and TV off before disconnecting the video cable. ■

✱ USEFUL URLS

The following websites provide additional information on the topics covered in this chapter.

en.wikipedia.org/wiki/PictBridge outlines the PictBridge direct printing standard.

www.canon.com.au/about/press_room/story_830.html has a 'white paper' on PictBridge as a photo printing solution.

picasa.google.com.au/ links to Picasa, a free image downloading and organisation tool that includes basic image editing and viewing functions.

↗ **www.photoreview.com.au/guides for direct links.**

CHAPTER 11

Printing Digital Photos

Although some DSLR users will prefer the simplicity of having their photographs printed by a photolab, there are some powerful reasons for buying your own photo printer and printing at home. The latest printers are easy to operate and produce prints that are as good as – and often better than – photolab prints. They may also cost a lot less and prints tend to resist fading for much longer.

Provided the shot was taken with the top resolution and quality settings, printing at home is a simple and straightforward process. If you obtain disappointing results, check the resolution settings to ensure the files are large enough to print at the size you've selected (see the diagram in Chapter 1.)

Photo printers come in two types: inkjet and dye-transfer (or dye-sublimation). Both types can produce photo quality prints but inkjet printers are cheaper to run and capable of producing much larger prints. Most dye-transfer printers are restricted to snapshot-sized output, while inkjet printers span the range from snapshot to poster-sized – and larger. We'll focus on inkjet printers in this chapter as they are the most popular with keen photographers.

DESKTOP PRINTER OPTIONS

If you're looking for simplicity and portability, there are plenty of portable snapshot printers on the market that produce 10 x 15 cm prints. Most are PictBridge compatible (see Chapter 10) and some have card slots for direct printing (although not necessarily all card types). A few have viewing screens to make it easy to select shots for printing.

Family photographers are usually better off with a general-purpose A4 printer that can produce a range of output sizes. Affordably-priced high-quality 'photo' printers are available in both a single-purpose printer form and as part of a multi-function printer/copier/scanner unit. Many come with software for printing multiple copies of a photo on a single A4 sheet of paper. Some allow users to print their own photos as labels on specially-treated CDs and DVDs.

Most serious photographers will want a printer that accepts at least A3 size paper and many will require a model with roll paper capabilities for printing panoramas. These printers can be economical to run, particularly when making poster-sized prints. Many can also print on special 'fine art' papers that provide a 'quality' look to the picture.

A typical snapshot printer that uses dye-transfer technology. Direct printing from a digital camera is supported via a USB cable and images for printing can be selected via the camera's LCD screen.

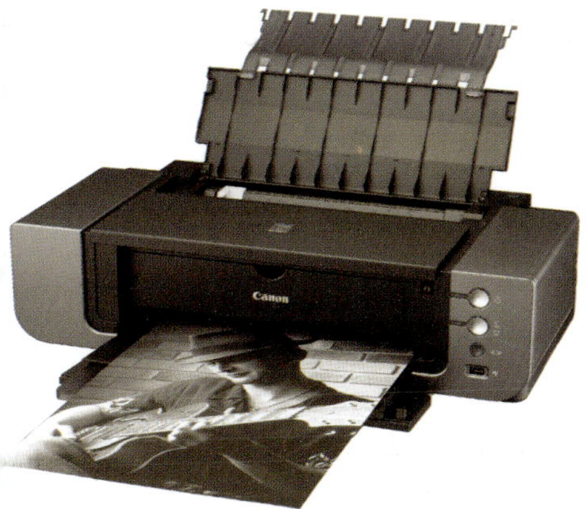

Serious photographers require a printer that can make poster-sized prints and produces very high picture quality.

BUYING TIPS

Choosing a photo printer is relatively straightforward – provided you know what to look for. The simplest printers use four ink colours: cyan, magenta, yellow and black. In theory, all other colours can be produced by combining these four colours in different proportions. In practice, however, no inks are totally colour-pure so four-ink printers are seldom fully photo-capable.

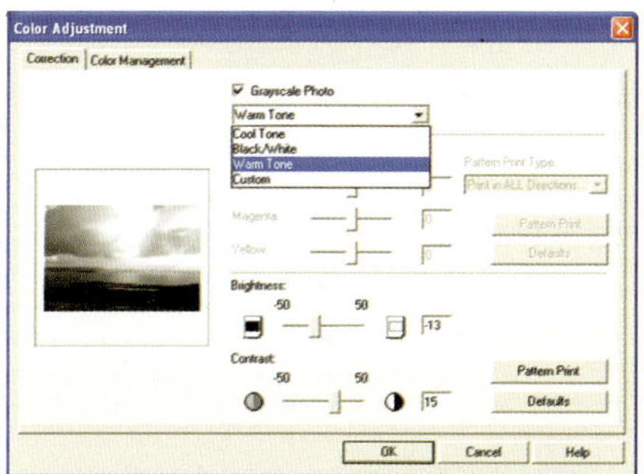

The ability to fine-tune tones and adjust brightness and contrast in the printer driver is important for B&W printing.

To produce the full range of tonal nuances, printer manufacturers have developed new ink sets with increased colour and tonal accuracy. The essential message is that the more inks a printer can use, the greater the subtlety of tonal nuance it is capable of – and the better the end result. Printers with six coloured inks produce more photo-like prints than those with four colours.

The same is true for black-and-white (B&W) printing, where the purest greys and subtlest tones can only be produced with at least one grey ink in the ink set. Special 'advanced' B&W drivers allow a higher degree of tonal fine-tuning. The real differences show up with enlargements at A3 size and over, especially in portraits.

Printer buyers should also look for printers that can work in the Adobe RGB colour space, which has a wider gamut (range) than the 'universal' sRGB colour space. The number of nozzles in the print head and the minimum picolitre size of the ink droplets will provide a good idea of the printer's ability to reproduce very fine detail.

PREPARING IMAGES FOR PRINTING

Just about any image editing software – and some other applications as well – can be used for printing photos, as long as it

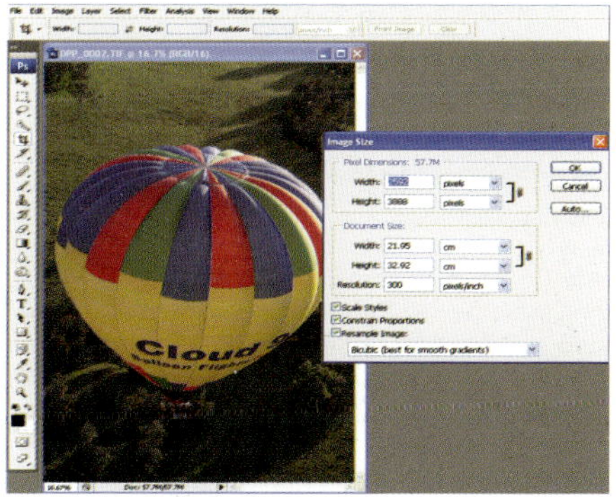

The Image Size dialog box in your editing software allows you to adjust the size of the picture and the output resolution before committing to a print.

interfaces correctly with the printer's driver and provides you with the functions you want to use. The former is particularly important as you normally need to set up the printer for the type of paper you are using via the printer driver.

Before starting to print you must determine how large the image should be. In Chapter 1 we showed the relationship between the sensor resolution of a digital camera, the maximum file size it produced and the recommended print size at 300 dots/inch (dpi), the ideal print resolution for most situations.

All printers come with driver software and most include a suite of software applications that may include a basic image editor and an organiser for cataloguing and viewing images. The printer driver allows the printer to interact with your computer and is normally installed from the supplied software disk before the printer is connected to a computer.

As well as allowing printer and PC to interact, printer drivers contain 'profiles' (or descriptions) of each type of paper that can be used with that printer. These profiles set the printer's operating parameters to match the requirements of the paper that is selected, giving the user the best possible chance of making colour-accurate photo prints. Because the profiles in each printer driver specify only the papers that carry the printer manufacturer's brand, photographers who wish to use third-party papers are forced to guess which paper setting in the driver is the best match for the paper they plan to use. This can be a hit-and-miss situation so it is generally best to use the printer manufacturers' inks and papers.

PRINTING VIA THE PRINTER DRIVER

Selecting 'Print' when you have a digital photo open in an image editor normally takes you to the printer driver. Printing a digital photograph usually involves most of the following steps – although they may not necessarily be the order in which we have presented them here.

1. Check that the correct printer has been selected.
2. Check the paper size and orientation, using the Page Layout control to adjust settings, if required.

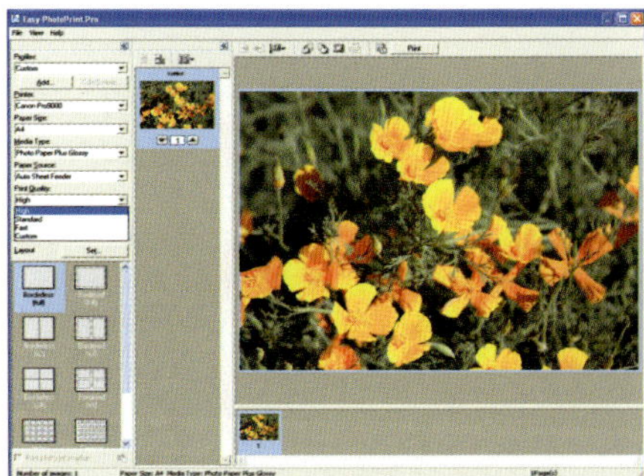

Most printer drivers allow users to set the output size and quality and choose whether prints will be produced with or without white borders. Some also allow multiple copies of the same image to be printed on a single sheet of paper.

3. Fit your image onto your paper, using the Output Size settings.
4. Click on 'Print' to go to the printer interface.
5. Click on 'Properties' to access the paper and printing settings.
6. Match the paper type to the paper you are using.
7. Select Print With Preview. This displays how the final print will look and allows you to check that the image is correctly positioned and sized. Note,

the image is usually displayed at low resolution so it may look grainy and its colours and brightness levels may not match the final print.

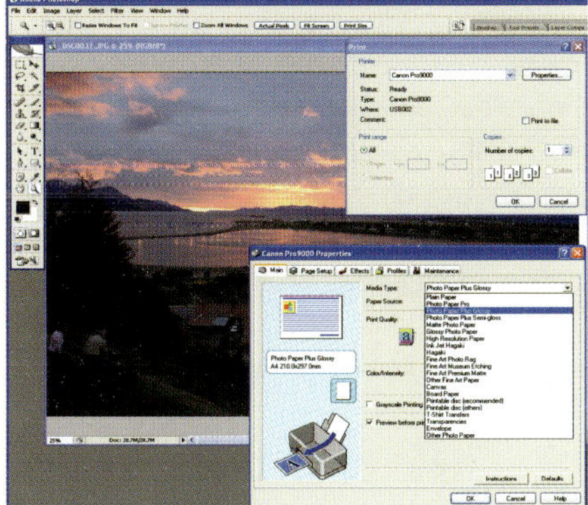

For the best-looking prints, it's vital to match the paper type in the printer driver to the paper you will print on.

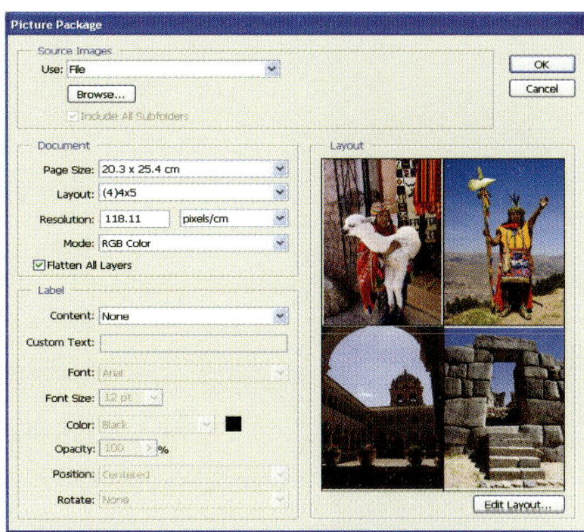

Some editing software applications help users to set up collections of images for printing on a single sheet of paper. This can be a great time saver and may reduce paper wastage.

Some software applications have settings for printing more than one photo on a single sheet of paper. Most allow users to create multiple copies of a single shot or import a selection of pictures and print them on a single sheet of paper. This software interfaces with the printer driver.

Some printers offer a range of additional settings, including greyscale and sepia options for monochrome prints plus hue, saturation and brightness adjustments. It is usually better to make most of these adjustments in the image editor before moving to the printer driver. The majority of printer drivers allow photographers to choose between 'borderless' prints, in which the image extends to the edges of the paper and prints with white borders.

Unfortunately, most inkjet papers have been produced in standard printing paper sizes so if you choose the 'borderless' printing setting, your photographs may not fit exactly on the paper when they are printed. This is particularly true for shots taken with 4:3 or 16:9 aspect ratios, which are best printed with borders. Previewing the image before printing (step 7) allows you to check the position of the image on the paper so you don't make prints with off-centre images or inappropriate cropping.

Most editing software – and many printer drivers – will allow you to scale the image to fit the paper you're using; just check the Scale to Fit Media box in the preview interface. In some applications you can also re-scale images by dragging out the corners until they fit on the paper as you want them. The driver can usually adjust the image data to produce high-quality prints unless a high degree of enlargement is involved.

HANDLING PRINTS

To minimise the risk of smearing, avoid touching the print surface as the print comes out of the printer. Wait for a minute or so before removing each print from the tray. Let the prints dry for about an hour before stacking them; and stack them with sheets of plain paper interleaved between the printed sheets so you avoid transferring any ink that may not have dried fully from one print to the next.

Inkjet prints will maintain their vibrant colours and tonal ranges for the longest time when they're protected from direct sunlight and airborne contaminants. The worst possible place to display them is on the refrigerator door, where they are subject to ozone and other damaging influences.

Have all prints that will go on display framed behind glass or encapsulated in plastic ('laminated') before they go on display. Choose photo albums with acid- and lignin-free pages and covers and glassine interleaving if you want your stored prints to last as long as possible. ∎

✱ USEFUL URLS

The following websites provide additional information on the topics covered in this chapter.

www.photoreview.com.au/pocketguides/printing-digital-photos-pocket-guide-4th-edition.aspx links to Photo Review's latest Printing Digital Photos Pocket Guide.

www.photoreview.com.au/tips/outputting/optimising-printing-efficiency.aspx provides advice on saving money when printing digital photos.

www.normankoren.com/digital_tonality.html provides an excellent series of guides to digital printing, covering monitor calibration, image editing, colour management and printing.

www.computer-darkroom.com/ provides tutorials in image editing, product reviews and feature articles and essays on printing and image editing. .

↗ **www.photoreview.com.au/guides for direct links.**

CHAPTER 12

Software and Accessories

New camera buyers often overlook the software that is supplied with a digital camera. However, it's an important part of the overall package because it can help you to get the most out of your camera in a number of different ways. All DSLRs are supplied with a software CD, which usually contains an image file browser and raw file conversion software. Raw file converters range from very basic browser-type applications that only allow users to view raw images and convert them into JPEG or TIFF format to those which provide a full range of adjustments as part of the conversion process.

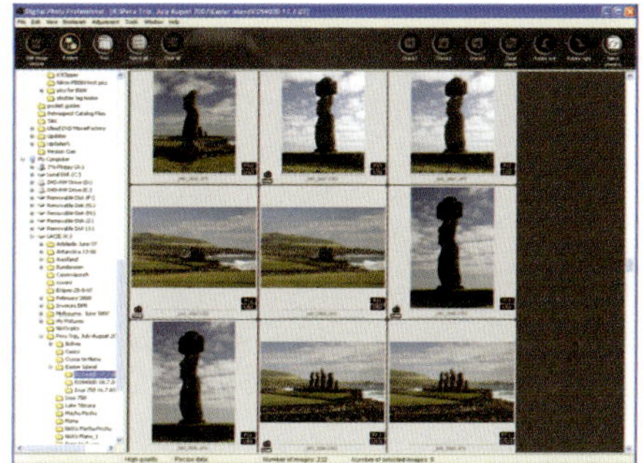

The browser/viewer interface in Canon's Digital Photo Professional software, which is supplied with all Canon DSLR cameras.

Some software disks also contain a combined viewing/downloading application which catalogues files as they are downloaded and allocates them to folders. These are usually identified by the date and time of the download.

Basic viewer/downloading applications usually allow users to view thumbnails in various sizes and display full images and enlarged shots. You can tag shots with star ratings for sorting, rotate shots and view slideshows with a selection of transition effects. It may also be possible to email and print shots directly from the user interface.

Some manufacturers include multi-lingual versions of the camera user's manual in PDF format. Others provide simple editing and/or panorama stitching applications. Professional cameras are often supplied with software for using the camera when it is connected ('tethered') to a computer, wireless transmission support or GPS data tagging facilities. But the most critical application for photographers who want to get the most from their DSLRs is the raw file converter.

Canon's EOS Digital Solution Disk also includes a Picture Style Editor that allows users to create their own Picture Style files, which can be uploaded to the camera. Adjustments are provided for colour tone, colour saturation, contrast and sharpness. Photographers can also fine-tune specific colours

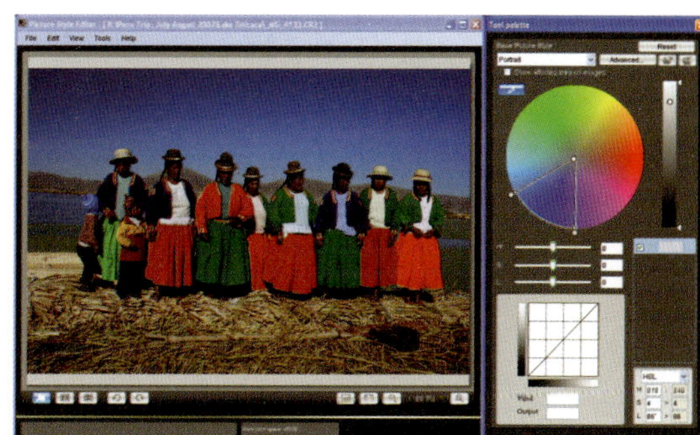

Canon's Picture Style Editor allows photographers to change Picture Style modes, adjust the settings used to create a shot and save new Picture Styles for future use.

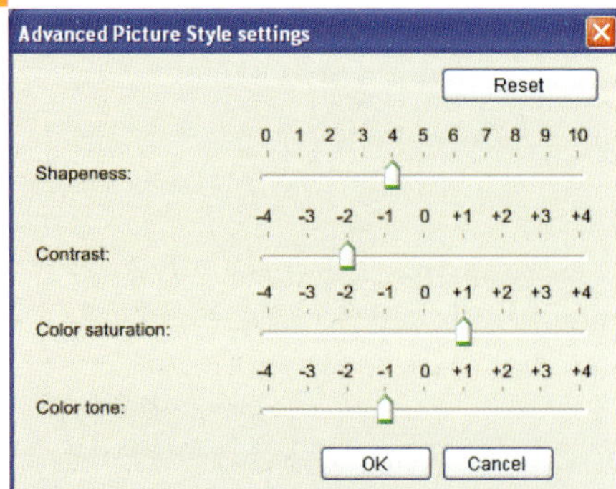

Fine-tuning is provided for sharpness, contrast, colour saturation and colour tone.

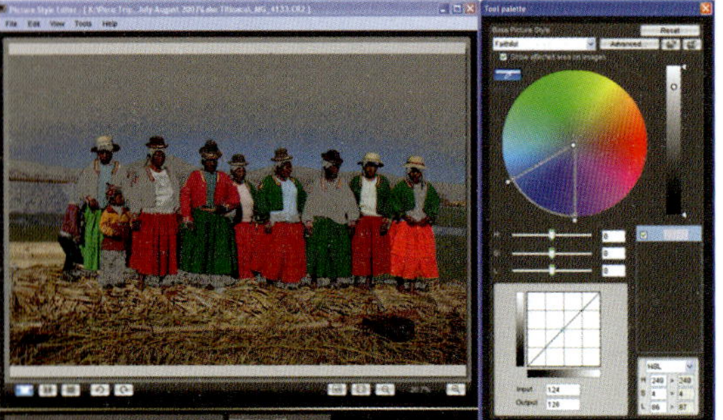

Clicking on the Show Affected Area on images box on the Tool palette lets users see which parts of the image will be affected before making changes.

by adjusting hue, saturation and luminosity, as well as changing the tone curve.

Up to 100 colour adjustment points can be specified and tweaked via three display modes: RGB, LAB and HSL. Sets of adjustments can be saved as Picture Style files with the *.PF2 extension for registration and use in any Canon camera that includes the Picture Style function. Currently, this software only supports raw images shot with cameras released after July 2007 but future versions will support future models – although no reverse compatibility to older EOS models is planned.

Some software bundles – or applications in them – include printing software that integrates with the drivers of most popular photo printers.

BUNDLED RAW FILE CONVERTERS

Bundled raw file converters vary from powerful, intuitive and easy to use programs to with limited capabilities that are downright frustrating. A good raw file converter will integrate effectively with your workflow - and your favourite editing software. This integration should include a raw file browser and the ability to apply settings from one image to a group of other images.

Some manufacturers develop their own raw conversion software in-house, while others use third-party applications that have been adjusted to work with the proprietary data. In-house programs usually integrate more effectively with the camera's data and settings. Nobody knows an image file better than the engineers who designed the camera!

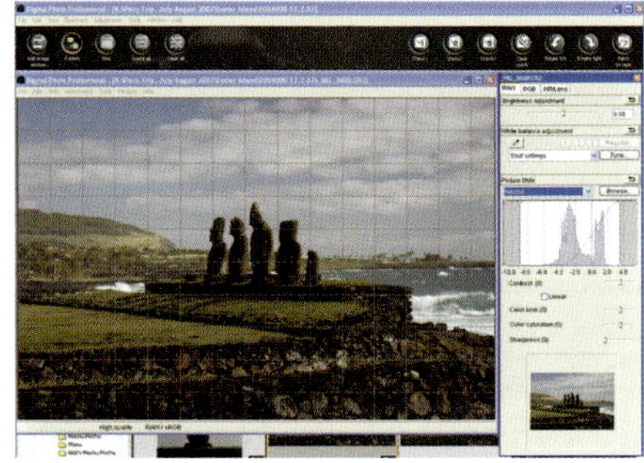

Canon's Digital Photo Professional provides a full range of adjustments for CR2.RAW files and supports 16-bit TIFF conversion.

Proprietary raw converters are designed specifically for the manufacturer's cameras and may support one, several or all models in the range. Updates are often provided when new cameras are added. Since these updates may include additional functions and/or fixes to known problems they are worthwhile having. (Check the manufacturer's website for details.)

While the raw file converters supplied with DSLR cameras generally allow photographers to convert raw images into 16-bit TIFF files, care must be taken when selecting an image editing application for further adjustments. The simplest image editors are usually restricted to 8-bit files so DSLR photographers who plan to shoot raw files can only work with the more sophisticated applications.

EDITING SOFTWARE

Applications that support 16-bit TIFF files include Adobe's Photoshop and the latest versions of Photoshop Elements; ACDSee Pro 2, Corel Paint Shop Pro and PhotoImpact (both of which are distributed by Corel) and The GIMP. Photoshop is a professionally-priced package and the others are affordably-priced (or free).

Paint Shop Pro and Photo Impact both contain basic raw file converters, while a free plug-in, Adobe Camera Raw, is available for Photoshop and Photoshop Elements to provide powerful raw file conversion facilities. The GIMP is a freeware application without raw file conversion capabilities.

While freeware applications are often very capable, the level of support is negligible, whereas purchased products tend to provide a high degree of online support and are better for photographers with minimal computer experience.

Most of the above applications are available as trial downloads from the developers' websites. Try-out times range from 15 to 30 days, during which time you can use the software for free. When the trial period expires, you will be offered the opportunity to purchase the application.

ACCESSORIES

Accessories can expand your shooting capabilities and greatly enhance the satisfaction you can gain from owning a DSLR camera. Most manufacturers offer a wide selection of accessories including lenses, flash units, image storage devices, remote controllers, rechargeable batteries and lens filters. Some also include wireless file transmitters to transfer images wirelessly, interchangeable focusing screens (for cameras that accept them), cables for connecting a GPS device and data security systems.

We've already covered lens options in Chapter 3 so in this chapter we'll look at some of the other accessories you could add to your kit.

Accessory flash units allow photographers to attach a light source to the camera for use in situations where more light is required for a

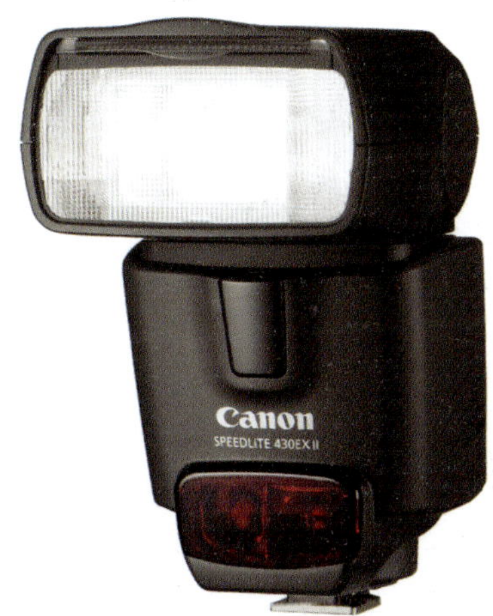

Canon's Speedlite 430EX II is a good choice for keen photographers as it provides a huge increase in light output with a wide range of controls.

www.photoreview.com.au ■ DIGITAL SLR POCKET GUIDE

correct exposure – or to allow the photographer to take the shot with the desired lens aperture setting without risking camera shake. They are also required by professional cameras which lack a built-in flash.

Although the flash unit requires its own battery (or batteries), the hot-shoe fitting allows it to connect electronically with the camera to support TTL (through-the-lens) flash exposure metering. This shuts off the flash light when the correct amount of light has been delivered for the camera settings.

Flash units come in varying sizes, with different light emission levels. The 'power' of a flash is indicated by its Guide Number (GN), which defines the illumination range in feet and/or metres at a specified ISO setting (usually ISO 100). Many flash units have adjustable heads for 'bouncing' the light off ceilings, walls or other reflective objects to provide a 'softer' illumination.

Some cameras allow several flash units to be synchronised for multiple-flash set-ups. Special 'ring' flash units are available for macro shooting.

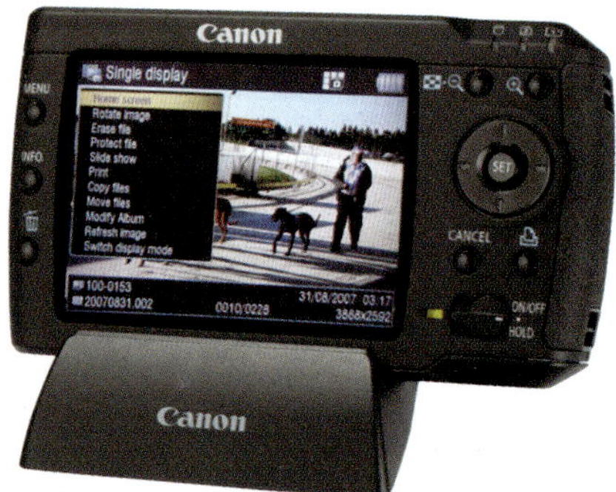

A portable storage device allows photographers to store the contents of many memory cards and also provides viewing and file organisation facilities.

They produce even illumination around the subject and are ideal for scientific and technical applications.

Image storage devices are valuable for travelling photographers as they provide back-up facilities for downloading files from the memory cards used for picture-taking. Consisting of a laptop hard disk drive in an enclosure, they usually include a LCD screen for managing file transfers and viewing stored images and can display both JPEG and raw files.

Once the files have been transferred you can usually sort them into albums where you can view single images, index thumbnails and slideshows. Some can also play video clips and/or audio files. A few storage devices support direct printing via a USB cable but image editing is not provided. Typical storage capacities range from about 40GB to 100GB, with prices increasing with capacity.

Remote controllers allow you to trigger the camera's shutter from a distance. Two types are available, wireless and direct. Wireless controllers work with radio waves while direct controllers are plugged into a socket on the camera and operated via a switch.

Controllers have two main advantages:
1. They allow the shutter to be triggered without jiggling the camera or affecting the subject.
2. They allow the shutter to be kept open for more than 30 seconds when the camera is in Bulb mode.

Wireless file transmitters are special tools that provide high-speed transfer of image files from the camera to an FTP server where they are saved. Usually made only for professional cameras, they are a particularly valuable tool for photojournalists and sports photographers, although studio photographers also find them

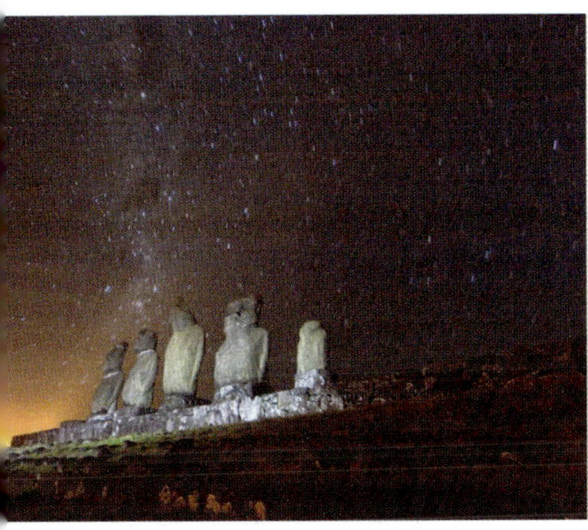

A remote controller is required for photographing star trails. The camera's shutter is set for a Bulb exposure and held open for the required exposure time (in this case, 30 minutes) before the controller is used to close it again.

handy for transferring image files to a computer quickly.

The main advantage of wireless file transfer is the flexibility it provides. Photographers can move about on a location or in a studio and download images as they shoot without requiring the camera to be connected to a computer. They can also shoot RAW+JPEG files and send only the JPEGs.

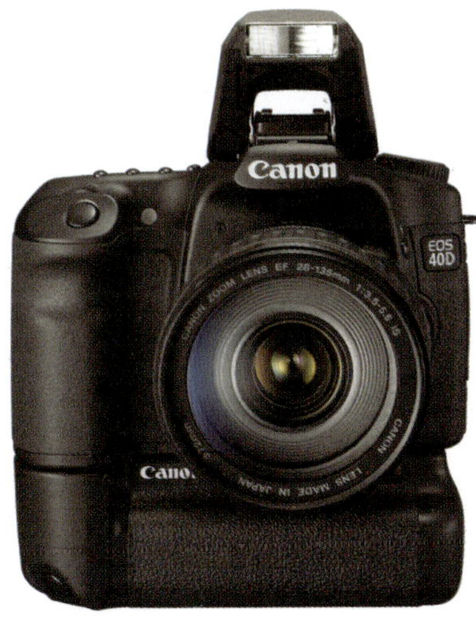

A pro-sumer DSLR with a vertical battery grip attached to its base.

Because image files can be viewed immediately after they are captured, a wireless file transmitter will speed up a photographer's workflow. Transferred shots can be selected on a PC by an editor and displayed for review or sent on to newspaper offices. This setup is highly effective for workflow speed in sports, news and other fields where response time is crucial.

Another popular accessory is a vertical battery grip, which are handy for shooting portraits. Most DSLR manufacturers offer these for the professional and pro-sumer models in their ranges. A capacious camera bag is handy for carrying all your equipment. Some camera manufacturers include one or two bags in their product ranges but specialist manufacturers make and supply most products in this market. ■

✱ USEFUL URLS

The following websites provide additional information on the topics covered in this chapter.

www.photoreview.com.au carries regular reviews of a wide range of accessory products.

www.adobe.com/downloads/ offers trial downloads of software applications such as Photoshop, Photoshop Elements and the latest Camera Raw plug-ins for raw file conversion.

web.canon.jp/imaging/picturestyle/index.html provides details of Canon's Picture Style settings and the Picture Style Editor. It also has additional Picture Styles that can be downloaded.

web.canon.jp/imaging/speedlite/index.html provides information on the latest Canon Speedlites.

web.canon.jp/imaging/osk/index.html outlines Canon's Original Data Security Kit and the cameras it can be used with.

web.canon.jp/imaging/wft/index.html contains information about Canon's Wireless File Transmitters..

↗ **www.photoreview.com.au/guides for direct links.**

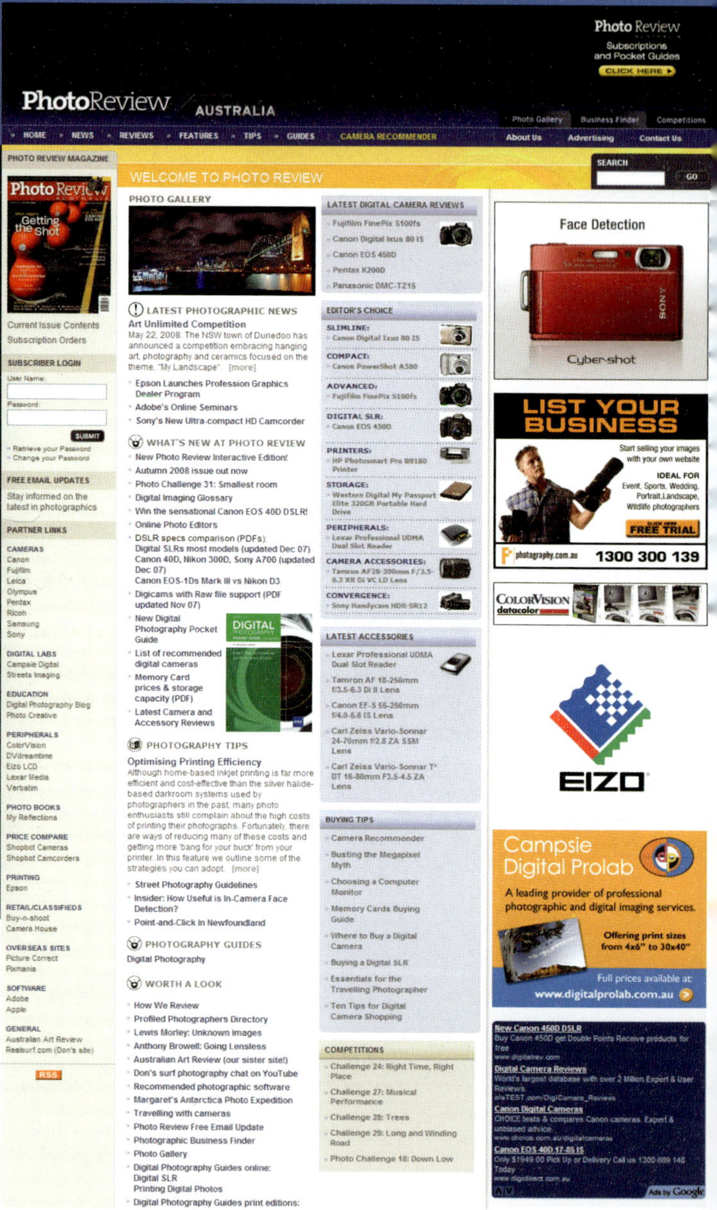

Digital Imaging Glossary

A guide to common terms associated with digital photography.

AE and AF Locks: Button controls on a camera that allow photographers to lock the exposure on a different part of the subject from the point of focus – or vice versa. In most cameras, pressing the shutter button halfway down locks both the AE (auto exposure) and AF (autofocus) settings.

Ambient Light: The light that exists in a specific situation without augmentation with flash or studio lights. Also known as 'available light'.

Aperture: The opening in the iris diaphragm of a lens that allows light to pass through the lens to the image sensor.

Aperture-priority: Usually denoted by the A (or Av) setting on a camera's mode dial, this shooting mode allows the photographer to set a specific aperture value while the camera will adjust the shutter speed automatically to ensure a correct exposure. The main purpose of this shooting mode is to control depth-of-field.

APS-C: A term originally developed for the 'Advanced Photo System' film format but now used to define a digital imaging sensor size that measures between 21.5 x 14.4 mm and 23.7 x 15.7 mm in area.

Archiving: Preserving digital images in a way that is independent of where these records are kept. Image archives can consist of prints or copies on optical disk or hard disk drive.

Artefacts: Undesirable visual defects produced by digital imaging systems. They can be generated by either input or output devices and include noise, colour casts, distortions and lost information. All degrade image quality.

Aspect Ratio: The relationship between the horizontal and vertical dimensions of an image. The horizontal dimension is normally quoted first. A 35mm film frame has an aspect ratio of 3:2, as do most DSLR cameras. Images from Four Thirds System DSLRs and compact digicams have a 4:3 aspect ratio. Many digital cameras and camcorders also offer a 'widescreen' format with a 16:9 aspect ratio.

Autofocus (AF): A camera control that focuses the lens on the subject. Two types of AF are in common use, active infrared (IR) and passive contrast-based. The former fires a beam of infrared light at the subject and calculates its distance on the basis of the return reflection; while the latter evaluates distance on the basis of image contrast (close subjects have higher contrast than their background). Many cameras include servo-AF systems that can focus on a moving subject. This is also known as 'focus tracking'.

Barrel Distortion: A type of image distortion that expands the central dimensions of the picture without affecting the periphery. It is most common in wide-angle lenses.

Bit: Short for 'binary digit', a bit is the smallest piece of information that can be handled by a computer and has a value of 0 or 1.

Bit Depth: The number of bits (binary digits) used to specify the brightness or colour range of each pixel in an image sensor. JPEG images are always recorded with 8-bit depth, which can record 256 (28) levels of red, green and blue. Cameras that support raw file capture offer higher bit depths, usually ranging from 12 to16 bits.

Bitmap: A file format that records image data as individual pixels. Denoted by the .bmp extension.

Blooming: The halo effect that occurs at borders between dark and light image tones due to an overflow of electrical charge that is generated by excessive light exposure on part or all of the image sensor.

Bracketing: An exposure technique that involves taking a series of shots with slightly different camera settings from those determined by the camera's automatic measurements. Most cameras provide bracketing controls for exposure and some also provide white balance and focus bracketing.

Buffer Memory: A special RAM storage area in a digital camera's memory system where image data is held while it awaits processing and transfer to the camera's memory card. A large buffer memory is required to support high-speed continuous shooting, especially at high image resolution.

Burst (Continuous) Shooting: A function that allows a camera to record a number of sequential shots in rapid succession. The number of frames that can be captured depends on the image resolution and the size of the buffer memory.

Centre-weighted Average Metering: An exposure metering pattern that integrates readings from all over the field of view, placing more emphasis on the centre of the field.

CCD (Charge-Coupled Device): A light-sensitive array of silicon cells that is commonly used for digital camera image sensors. It generates electrical current in proportion to light input and allows the simultaneous capture of many pixels with one brief exposure.

CMOS (Complementary Metal-Oxide Semiconductor): The alternative sensor array to CCD. CMOS sensors are cheaper to manufacture and use less power. Most digital SLR cameras have CMOS image sensors, while the majority of digicams use CCD technology.

Colour Filter Array: A mask, made of thin layers of dye that is applied over a digital camera sensor to enable it to record colour information. The individual colour patches filter out all but the chosen colour for that photosite and software interpolation is used to create a colour value for the resulting pixel based on surrounding pixel values. The most common filter pattern is the Bayer array, which uses alternating rows of red/green and green/blue patches (GRGB).

Colour: The value produced by combining luminance (brightness) and chrominance (colour) signals.

Colour Management: Setting up a combination of software and hardware devices to produce accurate colour reproduction through all stages of a digital imaging system - from capture to output.

Colour Space: A geometrical system used to describe a range of colours. Adobe RGB (1998) and sRGB are the most commonly used colour spaces in digital imaging.

CompactFlash (CF): A type of camera memory card that is commonly used in DSLR cameras. CF cards measure 43 x 36 mm in area and most are 3.3 mm thick. They come in capacities up to 64GB.

Compression: A mathematical processing system used to reduce the size of digital data files. Two types of compression are common in digital imaging: lossy (which sacrifices some data in order to obtain small files) and lossless (which involves little or no information loss).

Contrast: The difference between the lightest and darkest tones in an image. High-contrast images contain few steps between the lightest and darkest parts of the image, while low-contrast images contain many tonal gradations.

Crop: A manual or digital process that cuts away unwanted parts of an image.

Depth-of-Field: The area in a scene that appears acceptable sharp in a photographic image. Depth-of-field is controlled by the lens aperture. It is greatest with distant subjects, wide-angle lenses and small lens apertures and least with close subjects, telephoto lenses and large lens apertures. Some DSLR cameras have a dept-of-field preview button that temporarily closes the iris diaphragm so photographers can see the depth-of-field they will get in a shot.

Digital SLR (DSLR): A digital camera in which the subject is viewed through the same lens as the picture is taken with. A mirror is raised when the shutter button is pressed, allowing light to reach the image sensor. Most DSLR cameras use interchangeable lenses.

DPI (Dots Per Inch): The most commonly used unit of measurement for describing the resolution of digital image files for printing or scanning.

DPOF (Digital Print Order Format): Most digital cameras are compatible with the Digital Print Order Format (DPOF), a special type of metadata that lets users specify the photos they want printed by using the camera's menu system. The DPOF file is written to the camera's removable media, from which it can be read and executed by printing services and computer-based applications.

Dye-sublimation: A printing technology that uses dye-transfer to produce coloured prints. Most printers are restricted to snapshot-sized output.

Dynamic Range: The measurable difference between the brightest highlight and darkest shadow area in an image that can be reproduced by an imaging system.

Effective Pixels: The number of pixels that are actually used to capture the image (as distinct from the total pixel count for the sensor). The remaining pixels (the difference between total and effective pixels) are used to provide a 'dark current reading' so the camera has a black reference point. The number of unused pixels is at the camera manufacturer's discretion, which is why effective pixel count is the only reliable guide to the camera's resolution potential.

Exposure: A term used to describe the combination of lens aperture and shutter speed that delivers a pre-determined amount of light to the image sensor. All cameras include exposure meters, which measure the tones in the subject according to a selected pattern.

Exposure Compensation: A camera setting that allows photographers to over-ride the settings used by the camera to reduce or increase the overall exposure value. The control is indicated by a +/- icon, either on a button or in a menu.

Exposure Value (EV): A number determined by the brightness of the subject and the sensitivity selected for the recording medium, it is larger for bright subjects and smaller for dark ones. When the amount of light doubles, the EV increases by 1, making the value equivalent to one stop of exposure.

Fast lenses: Lenses with large maximum apertures – typically f/1.8 to f/2.8. Because they require more – and better quality – glass, fast lenses command premium prices.

File Format: The way in which digital information is saved by a software application. The most commonly used file formats for digital imaging are JPEG, TIFF and BMP (bitmap). Raw files are proprietary and, often, unique to each camera. Special software is required to decode raw files.

Filters: Add-on accessories that are used to change the appearance of digital images as they are recorded.

Flare: An imaging problem cause by light scatter within a lens. It is commonly seen in photographs of backlit subjects and may show up as bright or coloured spots on the subject or an overall reduction in contrast. Flare is reduced by coating the lens elements and using a lens hood to prevent stray light from entering the lens.

Flash Synchronisation: A control that ensures the flash is fired when the camera's shutter is open. Modern cameras often offer several flash synch settings; typically slow synch, which engages a slow shutter speed to allow background details to be recorded, first-curtain synch, which fires the flash just after the shutter opnes and rear-curtain synch, which fires the flash just before the shutter closes.

Four Thirds System: A digital SLR system developed by Olympus, Kodak and Panasonic that centres on an image sensor size of 18.0 x 13.5 mm and uses a special, non-propriteary lens mount.

'Full Frame' Sensor: An image sensor measuring 36 x 24 mm in area – which has the same surface area as a 35mm film frame.

Gamma: The technical term used to describe image contrast, it refers to the slope of the line that represents image output values versus image input values. It is applicable to both film-based and digital images.

Gamut: The range of colours that an image contains or an output device can reproduce.

Graduated Filters: Graduated filters are filters with variable light transmission. Typically half of the filter area is darker or a different colour while the rest is clear. They are used to darken overly-bright skies to ensure scenic shots have a natural balance between sky and land tones.

Highlight & Shadow Alerts: Playback settings that allow images to be displayed with blinking highlights and/or shadows so photographers can see whether shots have been correctly exposed.

Histogram: A graphical display that shows the distribution of tones within an image. The horizontal co-ordinate represents the possible pixel values from black to white, while the vertical co-ordinate shows the number of pixels in the image at each value.

Hue: The component of colour that relates to a specific wavelength or CIE co-ordinates.

Image Noise: A reduction in image quality that is usually seen as graininess and/or tiny white and coloured dots. It is caused by random fluctuations in the digital signal and associated with high ISO sensitivity settings and long exposure times.

Image Processor: The computer chip in a digital camera that converts the analogue signal from the image sensor into a digital picture.

Image Sensor: The element in a digital camera that records the digital image. Two types are popular: Charge-Coupled Devices (CCD) and Complementary Metal-Oxide Semiconductor (CMOS). CCDs are universally used in compact digicams while CMOS sensors are more common in DSLR cameras.

Image Stabilisation: A system for reducing the effect of camera shake. Two technologies are in common use, one compensating by moving elements in the lens and the by moving the sensor. The former is more effective.

Inkjet: A type of printer that applies microscopic ink droplets to paper to form images, graphics or text.

Internal Focusing (IF): A system for focusing a lens by moving internal elements. It allows the lens to remain the same length and its barrel does not rotate while focusing occurs, allowing angle-critical accessories like polarisers and graduated filters to be used.

Interpolation: A mathematical re-sampling technique that is used to alter the size of an image file by creating or removing pixels on the basis of existing pixel values. Some quality is sacrificed as a result of the interpolation process, particularly if files are made larger.

Iris diaphragm: The structure controlling the aperture in a camera's lens. The ratio between the diameter of this aperture and the focal length of the lens is given in an f/number.

ISO: The International Standards Organisation's system for defining sensor sensitivity. The system works by doubling. ISO 200 is double the sensitivity of ISO 100 and half the sensitivity of ISO 400.

JPEG: The image file format developed by the Joint Photographic Experts Group and denoted by the '.jpg' extension.

Kelvin (K): Colour 'temperature' is measured on a Kelvin scale, in which colours are denoted by the temperatures at which a heated black-body radiator matches the colour of the light source. This system allows precise colour values to be specified.

Lag: A term denoting delay after an action has been initiated. The most common lag times in digital imaging include shutter lag, autofocus (AF) lag and processing lag. Shutter lag describes the time taken for the camera to capture the shot after the shutter release has been pressed. AF lag defines the time it takes the camera to autofocus and processing lag describes the time images take to be processed and transferred to the memory card so the next image can be captured.

Landscape: A camera mode that sets the lens focus to near infinity, selects a small lens aperture and cancels the flash. For printing, the term defines a page orientation that is wider than it is high.

LCD (Liquid Crystal Display): LCD screens are used in digital cameras to preview and review shots. In some cameras they replace the optical viewfinder. Most also provide access to the camera controls via a set of menus, which are called up on screen and selected by pressing a button. Some cameras have separate LCD screens that display status information, such as frame counts, camera settings and battery power.

Lens: The optical device consisting of several glass elements which transmits and refracts light to produce the image that is recorded by a camera's sensor. DSLR cameras use interchangeable lenses.

Live View: A function on all compact digicams and many recent DSLR cameras that allows the LCD monitor to be used for composing photographs.

Manual: The Manual (M) setting on a camera's mode dial gives the photographer full control over the lens aperture and shutter speed settings.

Megapixels: A term used to describe one million pixels. It is used to define the number of pixels in a digital image and also (erroneously) to express the number of photosites in the image sensors in digital cameras.

Metadata: Structured data, stored with digital image files, which explains, locates, describes or otherwise makes using the original primary data more effective or efficient. Two types of metadata are important for digital camera users: the Exif standard and the Digital Print Order Format (DPOF) standard.

Monochrome: Refers to an image that is all one colour, typically black and white (with intermediate grey tones) or sepia. When images are recorded in monochrome, colour information is discarded.

Multi-pattern Metering: An exposure metering pattern that divides the subject area into five or more segments and individually evaluates the light levels within each segment. Exposure settings are determined by balancing the readings from each segment.

Noise: A random pattern of unwanted pixels that degrades the quality of image files.

Optical Zoom: The maximum zoom range achievable with the camera's lens. Image quality is fully maintained.

Orientation: The direction in which a page is printed: landscape is printed horizontally, while portrait is printed vertically.

Photosite: The light-sensitive cell on a digital image sensor, it records one intensity and one colour value. Information from several photosites is required to create a pixel in the image.

Pincushion Distortion: An image aberration that compresses the centre of the field.

Pixel: Short for 'picture element', this term describes the basic component of a digital image. Individual pixels are generally square and carry one value for colour, luminance and intensity. Millions of pixels are required to produce a digital image that approaches photographic quality.

Playback Zoom: A camera function that enables photographers to enlarge part of an image during playback to check focusing and exposure levels.

Polarisers or Polarising Filters: Polarising filters are used to reduce the effects of scattered light and, thereby, brighten colours and allow blue skies to be reproduced with a natural appearance. They can also reduce the effect of specular reflections off water or other shiny surfaces. Two types are available: linear and circular. Circular polarisers are recommended for photography.

PPI (Pixels Per Inch): Often used interchangeably with DPI to describe the resolution of a digital image.

Prime Lens: A lens that covers only one focal length.

Pro-sumer: Between professional and consumer (usually referring to camera equipment).

Raw Data: Digital information that has not been processed or formatted.

Raw Files: Raw files contain the image data as it is captured by the camera's sensor with only minimal processing applied. Many high-end digital cameras provide a raw capture option, most using proprietary file formats that require special software to decode. Because they are un-processed, raw files are effectively 'digital negatives'.

Resolution: The ability to reproduce fine detail - or the amount of detail in the image.

RGB: A colour model based on the red, green and blue components in the output, it is typically used for images that will be displayed on monitors.

Saturation: The intensity of a hue. Pastels have low saturation, while bright colours are highly-saturated.

Secure Digital (SD): A type of camera memory card that is used in some DSLR cameras. SD cards measure 32 x 24 x 2.1 mm and come in capacities up to 32GB. A high-capacity version, SDHC (Secure Digital High Capacity) was launched in 2006 and offers faster data transfer speeds.

Sharpening: An image enhancement technique that gives more distinct edges to subject areas, lines and tones in a digital image. Sharpening can be applied in the camera or in editing software.

Sharpening Artefacts: Defects introduced by in-camera sharpening systems. These generally appear as white or black halos around high-contrast areas in the subject and can sometimes be minimised by turning off the auto sharpening function in the camera.

Shutter Priority: Usually denoted by the S (or Tv – for time value) setting on a camera's mode dial, this shooting mode allows the photographer to set a specific shutter speed while the camera will adjust the lens aperture automatically to ensure a correct exposure. The main purpose of this shooting mode is to control the ways in which motion is depicted. Fast shutter speeds are used to 'freeze' movement, while slow shutter speeds record movement as a blur.

Spot Metering: An exposure metering pattern that takes a single reading from a small section of the field of view.

Telephoto: A term used for lenses with focal lengths greater than 70mm.

Thumbnail: A reduced-size, low-resolution version of a digital image, used mainly for sorting and retrieving image files.

TIFF (Tagged Image File Format): An image file format based on bitmapping that involves little or no data compression. Denoted by the .tif extension.

Tungsten Lighting: Light produced by either photofloods or domestic illumination, it has a Kelvin value of 3200 and is warmer than normal daylight.

USB (Universal Serial Bus): The most common way of connecting a peripheral device to a computer, USB offers 'hot' plug and play (you don't need to power-down the PC). The latest version USB 2.0 is significantly faster than the original USB 1.0 and USB 2.0 Hi-Speed is even faster.

VGA (Video Graphics Array): A video monitor with 640 x 480 pixel resolution. Also applied to 640 x 480 pixel images.

White Balance: The control on a digital camera used to adjust the colour balance of the image to make shots look natural under a variety of different lighting conditions. Most cameras have pre-sets for tungsten and fluorescent room lighting plus daylight and open shade. A few also include a flash setting. Virtually all digital cameras have an auto white balance setting.

Zoom: A camera or software control that causes the image - or part of it - to appear larger (zooming in) or smaller (zooming out).

Zoom lens: A lens that covers a range of focal lengths. Zoom lenses are usually several stops slower than prime lenses, particularly at longer focal lengths.